CHERISHED

LIBRARY
BOOK HOUSE
BRIGHTON

Gabriel N Cha

SCOTLAND
a Very
Peculiar History

Volume 1

Lean gu dluth ri cliu do shinnsre.
(Let us follow in the brave path
of our ancestors.)
Gaelic proverb.

To A, and my ancestors,
with love and thanks.

FMacD

Editor: Jamie Pitman
Published in Great Britain in MMIX by
Book House, an imprint of
The Salariya Book Company Ltd
25 Marlborough Place, Brighton BN1 1UB
www.salariya.com

ISBN: 978-1-906370-91-6

SALARIYA
SCRIBO   BOOK HOUSE   SCRIBBLERS

© The Salariya Book Company Ltd MMIX
All rights reserved. No part of this publication may be reproduced, stored
in or introduced into a retrieval system or transmitted in any form, or by
any means (electronic, mechanical, photocopying, recording or otherwise)
without the written permission of the publisher. Any person who does any
unauthorised act in relation to this publication may be liable to criminal
prosecution and civil claims for damages.

9 11 12 10 8

A CIP catalogue record for this book is available
from the British Library.

Printed and bound in China.
Printed on paper from sustainable sources
Reprinted in MMXVIII

This book is sold subject to the conditions that it shall not, by way of trade or
otherwise, be lent, resold, hired out, or otherwise circulated without the
publisher's prior consent in any form or binding or cover other than that in
which it is published and without similar condition being imposed on the
subsequent purchaser.

Visit
www.salariya.com
for our online catalogue and **free** fun stuff.

WARNING: The Salariya Book Company accepts no responsibility
for the historical recipes in this book. They are included only for their
historical interest and may not be suitable for modern use.

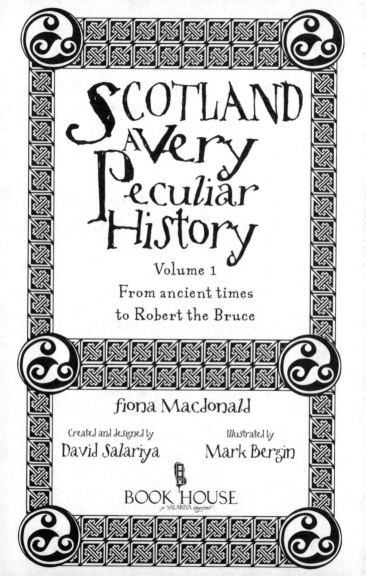

SCOTLAND
A Very Peculiar History

Volume 1

From ancient times
to Robert the Bruce

Fiona Macdonald

Created and designed by
David Salariya

Illustrated by
Mark Bergin

BOOK HOUSE
a SALARIYA imprint

'There is a great peculiarity about the Highlands and Highlanders...'
Queen Victoria
(English/German, 1819–1901)

'I have been trying all my life to like Scotchmen, and am obliged to desist from the experiment in despair.'
Charles Lamb
(English, 1775–1834)

'Much may be made of a Scotchman – if he be caught young.'
Dr Samuel Johnson
(English, 1709–1784)

'O wad some Pow'r the giftie gie us To see oursels as others see us.'
Robert Burns
(Scottish, 1759–1796)

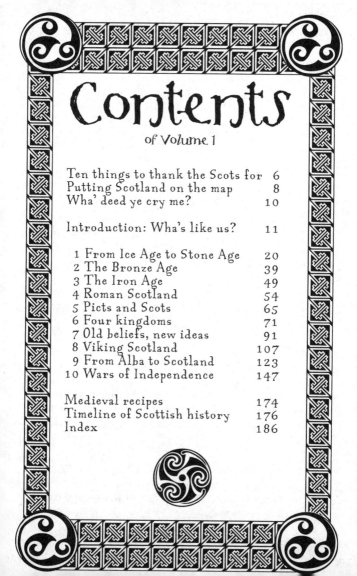

Contents

of Volume 1

Ten things to thank the Scots for

1. **Golf** 'Of this diversion the Scots are so fond, that when the weather will permit, you may see a multitude of all ranks, from the senator of justice to the lowest tradesman, mingled together in their shirts, and following the balls with the utmost eagerness.' (Scottish novelist Tobias Smollet, 1721–1771)

2. **Economics** 'The dismal science' was invented by famously eccentric Edinburgh professor Adam Smith (1723–1790). 'The real price of every thing…is the toil and trouble of acquiring it.'

3. **Science and technology** Scots invented logarithms, explained electromagnetism, discovered thermodynamics and created modern chemistry. They gave us medical breakthroughs from anaesthetics and antiseptics to kidney dialysis and ultrasound. They built boats, bridges, roads, railways, furnaces and steam engines. 'To measure is to know.' (William Thomson, Lord Kelvin, 1824–1907)

4. ***Encyclopaedia Britannica*** 'A dictionary of arts and sciences, compiled upon a new plan.' First compiled 1768–1781 in Edinburgh and still in print today.

5. **Whisky** 'Freedom and Whisky gang thegither!' (Robert Burns, 1786) 'Whiskey… loses its beneficial effect when taken in too large quantities.' (Lord Dunsany, 1878–1957)

6. **Bicycles** Invented by blacksmith Kirkpatrick MacMillan (1813–1878). The cheapest, most democratic, transport machine. 'Nothing compares to the simple pleasure of a bike ride.' (US President John F. Kennedy, 1917–1963)

7. **Waterproof coats, or 'macs'** Named after their Scots inventor, Charles Mackintosh (1766–1843). 'In Scotland there is no such thing as bad weather – only the wrong clothes.' (Billy Connolly, born 1942)

8. **Geology** The study of rocks and the earth's rotation was pioneered by James Hutton (1726–1797). 'Your country [Scotland] consists of two things, stone and water.' (Dr Samuel Johnson, 1709–1784)

9. **Environmental conservation** Pioneered by Scots-American John Muir (1838–1914): 'Nature loves man, beetles and birds with the same love.'

10. **Sherlock Holmes** Created by Scottish doctor Sir Arthur Conan Doyle (1859–1930): 'When a doctor goes wrong he is the first of criminals. He has the nerve and he has the knowledge.'

Putting Scotland on the map

1. c.3100 BC: Stone houses at Skara Brae
2. c.2500 BC: Stone circles at Brodgar and (2a) Callanish
3. c.1600 BC: Mummies at Cladh Hallan, South Uist
4. c 750 BC: Celtic hillfort at Eildon Hill
5. c.100 BC: Broch at Mousa
6. AD 84: Celts fight Romans at Mons Graupius
7. AD 122–143: Romans build Hadrian's Wall and (7a) Antonine Wall
8. AD 795–826: Vikings raid St Columba's monastery on Iona
9. AD 842: Cinead MacAlpin crowned king of Picts and Scots at Scone
10. 1297 and 1314: Scots defeat English invaders at Stirling Bridge and Bannockburn
11. 1513: Scots badly defeated at battle of Flodden
12. 1557–1558: Religious riots after Protestant Reformer John Knox returns to Edinburgh
13. 1692: Massacre at Glencoe; MacDonald clan members killed by Campbells loyal to London
14. 1746: Hanoverians defeat Jacobites at Culloden
15. 1759: Carron Ironworks opens
16. c.1780–1820: Edinburgh New Town built
17. 1853: Queen Victoria starts to build Balmoral Castle
18. 1877–1890: Rail bridges over the Forth and (18a) Tay
19. 1882: Crofters fight landowners for rights to land
20. 2004: New Scottish Parliament building opens

Key to cities:
- **A** Aberdeen
- **D** Dundee
- **E** Edinburgh
- **G** Glasgow
- **I** Inverness

Wha' deed ye cry me?*

They might all come from Scotland, but Scots, Scotch and Scottish – people and things – are not all the same!

- **Scots** is a language, spoken in the Lowlands.
- **Scotch** is an adjective, applied mostly to foodstuffs, such as whisky, beef, broth, eggs and pancakes. Traditionally, to call a person 'Scotch' was offensive – possibly because the word was mostly used by the English (it's a shortened, English, version of 'Scottish').
- **Scottish** is what the people of Scotland call themselves, and also their national institutions such as the Scottish Parliament.

But – just to keep you on your toes – the Church of Scotland is always the Church of Scotland. And a Scottish person living in Scotland is always a Scot.

* What did you call me?

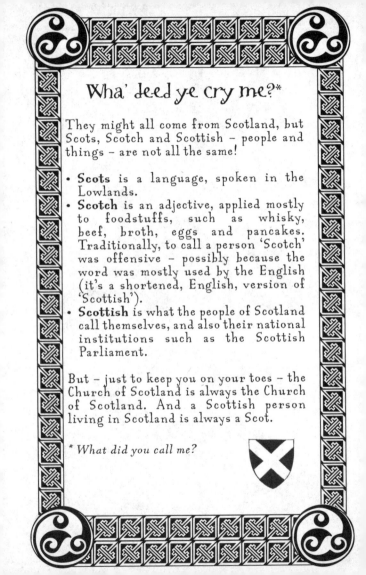

INTRODUCTION

Wha's like us?

Scotland is not a big country. It occupies just one-third of the land mass of Great Britain and its total area is only 78,783 square kilometres (30,418 square miles). It is surrounded on three sides by water; the coastline is so ragged that, stretched out, it would measure an astonishing 10,000 km (6,200 miles).

Scotland used to be much bigger, but around three-quarters of its surface was scraped away by glaciers during the past 13 million years. Its western side is still slowly rising from the sea now that it is no longer weighed down by unimaginable quantities of ice.

About two-thirds of Scotland is upland and mountains; most of it lies further north than Moscow. Scotland's northernmost region – the Shetland Isles – is closer to the Arctic Circle than to the south of Britain. But its western coast is washed by a warm ocean current – the Gulf Stream – and subtropical plants, such as palm trees, flourish in sheltered gardens there.

Scotland has some of the oldest rocks in the world (gneiss, found on the Isle of Lewis), the world's longest-lasting fogs (on Ben Nevis, Britain's highest mountain; they last for 300 days a year) and many extinct volcanoes. The strongest winds in Britain blow across it; the record is 277 kph (172 mph), on the summit of Cairn Gorm. There are villages shadowed by mountains which don't see the sun from November to February; in northern Scotland it stays light all night in May and June.

Scotland has 2,000 castles (many of them haunted), 790 islands, countless legendary monsters, a few real prehistoric fish (powan, in Loch Lomond) and the only national instrument – the bagpipes – to be legally recognised as a weapon of war.

Twelve Highlanders and a bagpipe make a rebellion.

Scottish proverb

Scotland may be small, but its people have big ideas, and Scotland has played a surprisingly powerful part in world history. Scottish people are famous – or infamous – for their rather prickly pride in their country and its achievements. It is no wonder that their national emblem is a particularly vicious variety of thistle.

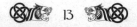

flower of Scotland

According to legend, thistles saved Scotland from invaders, and have been honoured ever since. In AD 973 a Viking fleet landed secretly, in the dark, at Luncarty, near Perth. Planning a surprise night attack on the sleeping Scottish soldiers, the Vikings took off their boots and shoes and tiptoed towards the Scots' camp. However, they did not get far. The seashore was thick with spiny thistles, and the startled Vikings could not help crying out in pain. The Scottish sentries heard them, and the Scottish army was saved!

Scottish pride has not made the Scots easy neighbours for the other kingdoms in Britain; as far back as AD 1702, Queen Anne, in London, was calling Scottish people 'unreasonable and strange'. But in reply, Scottish patriots list all that Scotland has given to the world, from golf and whisky to bicycles, raincoats, grand pianos, hot-blast furnaces, radar, television, antiseptics, kidney transplants, ultrasound scanners, Dolly the sheep and Nu-mice (bred to help study medical genetics) – not forgetting the *Beano* comic, and marmalade.

They praise famous past Scots such as Alexander Graham Bell (who invented the telephone, and much more besides), Alexander Fleming (one of the first to discover antibiotics), the philosopher David Hume (who revolutionised our understanding of the way people think), Elsie Inglis (who led teams of female doctors to work in World War I battlefields), Clementia Black (who campaigned for votes for women), Robert Burns (who wrote some of the best love-songs ever) and Andrew Carnegie (who made a vast fortune, but gave most of it away to charity) –

and hope that present-day Scots will continue this tradition of achievement.

Scotsmen working abroad were not idle. They commanded Russian imperial armies, took the first sheep to Australia and New Zealand, mapped Africa's great rivers, invented basketball (in Canada), built lighthouses in Japan, and one even served as official magician to French emperor Napoleon. For over 40 years, an actor of Scottish ancestry was the voice of Mickey Mouse.

Today, more people claiming Scottish ancestry live outside Scotland than in it. The population of Scotland is between 5 and 6 million; but around 13 million people of Scottish origin live in the USA and Canada, with millions more in Europe, Australia, New Zealand and many other parts of the world.

Scottish people have always been fascinated by their history. They play ancient sports, perform traditional music, speak historic languages, and are some of the few people in Europe still to wear traditional clothes and enjoy it. They eat traditional foods, such as haggis, that are unknown elsewhere in Britain, and celebrate historic festivals, such as Burns Night and Hogmanay, that are all Scotland's own. Even the rivalry of their two top football teams, Rangers and Celtic, is based on historic quarrels (see Volume 2).

This love of Scottish history is shared by millions of others. The world's first historical novels were written in Scotland by Sir Walter Scott (1771–1832), and were translated into many different languages. Surprisingly, they also inspired at least 40 operas. More recently, epic films *Chariots of Fire* (1981), about Scots sporting hero Eric Lidell, and *Braveheart* (1995), about Scots freedom-fighter William Wallace, both won multiple Oscars and made a fortune in box-office takings worldwide.

Every summer, around 16 million tourists from many different lands visit Scotland to admire its spectacular scenery, majestic old buildings and mysterious prehistoric monuments. They flock to Mods (music festivals), open-air Highland Games (sports festivals), go island-hopping (take ferry trips to misty, romantic islands), shelter from the rain and the midges (tiny black biting insects that live in bogs) and munch their way through tonnes of shortbread (in spite of its name, a sweet, crumbly biscuit, sold in tartan-patterned tins). Tourism and the heritage industry are now Scotland's biggest employers.

Two thousand years ago, Scottish chiefs kept bards (poets) to sing their praises and memorise family traditions. Who knows how many million words have been written, spoken or sung about the history of Scotland since then? This book looks at just a few of the less well-known – and perhaps unexpected – facts about Scotland's past. It's a very peculiar history…

Hear my song...

For thousands of years, in Gaelic, Scots and English, Scottish mothers have crooned gentle lullabies to babies, Scottish lovers have charmed their sweethearts with romantic serenades, and Scottish mourners have wept over sorrowful elegies. Scottish crowds have cheered at rousing Border ballads, Scottish dancers have jigged to lively *puirt a beul* (songs without words), Scottish ploughmen have hummed jaunty airs, and Scottish women weavers have kept time as they worked to cheerful – and sometimes rather rude – 'waulking' songs.

Since then, Scottish rock stars have topped the charts, Scottish ceilidh bands have set feet tapping, and Scottish football fans have roared out raucous chants and (alas) abusive, sectarian rhymes.

For over 200 years, lilting Scottish songs and haunting Scottish melodies have brought back wistful memories to Scots migrants all round the world. They have lamented hopeless but romantic Scottish heroes, such as Bonnie Prince Charlie, and conjured up enticing images of Scotland's wild beauty. Unlike traditional songs, which were never written down but memorised and passed on from singer to singer, these 'Dream of Scotland' songs were carefully composed, mostly in the 18th and 19th centuries. But that does not devalue their charm – or their nostalgic power.

fROM ICE AGE TO STONE AGE

c.750,000–2500 BC

The first human-like creatures arrive in the British Isles around 750,000 BC – but they don't venture as far as Scotland. They're happy to stay further south, where it's warmer.

750,000–18,000 BC

For hundreds of thousands of years, the climate keeps changing. Every few millennia, the seas around Scotland suddenly turn to solid ice – in a space of just 10 years! – and the surrounding land gets deep-frozen. It's not a safe place to stay!

Land bridge forms here due to falling sea levels as sea-water freezes

N

Scotland

Edge of ice sheet

Present-day coastline

The British Isles in the Ice Age

18,000 BC

It's the peak of the last Ice Age. Huge glaciers, 100 metres thick, spread southwards from the Arctic. Scotland has disappeared! It's completely buried under ice!

Actually, just a few of the very tallest mountain peaks stand out above the ice. Because they are not ground down by glaciers, they keep their jagged shape. You can still see them in the present day, for example on the Isle of Rum. The tiny plants and bacteria growing on them somehow manage to survive, and are now Scotland's oldest living creatures.

12,000–11,000 BC

For a while the weather gets warmer, and Scotland goes all slushy. The land is awash with melting ice-floes and retreating glaciers. Huge, roaring rivers scour deep valleys and scatter giant boulders.

Scotland's first truly human visitors splash in from Norway, or perhaps Russia. They are chasing reindeer, and find little else, apart from fish, to tempt them to settle. But they leave stone arrowheads behind them, at Islay and Orkney.

11,000–9600 BC
Scotland has a mini Ice Age, all of its own. Once again, it becomes a lifeless, frozen land.

8500 BC
At last the glaciers go away, but Scotland is a wilderness of bare rock, mud and puddles. It's not a welcoming environment, but summer visitors soon arrive, and these travellers are tough! They camp at Cramond, near Edinburgh, in tents of animal skin. They are armed with stone-tipped spears. They hunt fox and lynx for fur, and fierce brown bears. But the bears are hungry too…

7000–5000 BC
Now the climate is warm enough for animals and people to live in Scotland all year round. Trees grow quickly. Reindeer, huge wild oxen and wolves roam free. There are bushes with nuts and berries, tasty roots, shoots and mushrooms, fish in rivers and the sea…

Morag hadn't realised she'd invented the 'Arbroath smokie'.

Red hair

Scotland's first settlers brought genes that mutated over the years to create a typically British – and Scottish – appearance. When the Romans arrived in Britain, in 55 BC, they were surprised to see so many people with red hair; it was rare elsewhere in Europe. Even today, Scotland still has the largest proportion of redheads in the world.

No, these new visitors do not walk on water: until around 6000 BC, a 'bridge' of dry land links the British Isles to the rest of the continent. Other newcomers wade through shallow seas from north-west Europe, or paddle dug-out log canoes.

The first Scots get together in small family groups, and wander from place to place, hunting and trapping animals and going fishing. Scotland is now covered in dense, boggy woodland, so they live beside rivers or around the coast. They build 'benders' (little shelters) from branches to sleep in, and huddle in caves. They make clothes from skins and tools from stone, bone and antler. They tame the wolves and turn them into dogs. They gather astonishing quantities of wild foods, especially nuts and shellfish...

But what do they do with the leftovers? Surprisingly, for teenagers and twenty-somethings (few Stone-Age people live much longer than 30), the first Scots are very tidy-minded. Each group digs pits for its nutshells and seashells. On the Isle of Colonsay, for example, they bury hundreds of thousands in just one season, around 6700 BC. All round the coast, they pile up giant middens (refuse mounds) of seashells, maybe 30 metres long, after eating the salty, gritty, rubbery, squirming sea creatures – alive!

6000 BC
Disaster! When cliffs fall into the sea in Scandinavia, the east coast of Scotland is swamped by a giant tsunami, with waves 25 metres high!

Wee folk

Ignoring evidence found by archaeologists, historian David MacRitchie (1861–1925) wrote that the first inhabitants of Scotland were tiny, hairy, earth-coloured creatures. He believed that memories of them were preserved in traditional fairytales about elves and brownies.

5000–4000 BC

New settlers arrive in Scotland from the north-west of Spain. They are very brave and daring (or perhaps just very hungry). They travel in some of the world's first ocean-going boats across the Bay of Biscay and along the west coast of the British Isles.

Here's a mystery – what do the new settlers do when they arrive? Make love or fight wars? We do not know for sure.

The legend of Princess Scota

The first writers of history in Scotland were not bothered by facts or evidence. They preferred to tell a good story, especially if it made Scottish kings – who paid them – look important by linking them to famous civilisations long ago. But their stories also feature settlers from Spain.

According to the *Scotichronicon* (written around AD 1440), an Ancient Greek prince was banished from his homeland, together with his Egyptian wife, the lovely Princess Scota, and their sons. They journeyed north and found a new home in Spain. But one of their sons sailed on, first to Ireland and then to a country further north. He named it Scotia in honour of his mother.

A different version of this story tells how an Egyptian princess married the king of Portugal. Their daughter, Scota, wed the king of Ireland, and their sons invaded Scotland. The invaders called themselves 'Children of Scota', and gave their name to the country.

It was said that Princess Scota carried a huge stone slab[1] with her from the Holy Land.[2] If so, Scota must have been a giant or some kind of wonder-woman. The stone weighs over 150 kg, and when it was stolen by Scottish Nationalists in 1950, it took three strong men to move it.

1 The stone really exists; called the 'Stone of Destiny', it was used in solemn, sacred ceremonies bonding Scottish kings to their kingdom.
2 The countries today known as Israel, Jordan, Lebanon, Palestine and Syria.

Do the Spanish settlers

- Kill the hunter-gatherers?
- Take over their hunting grounds?
- Ignore them, and set up separate campsites?
- Capture them as slaves?
- Make friends, and choose hunter-gatherer women as wives?

We can't be certain, but modern DNA tests show that many of today's Scottish men are descended from the Spanish settlers – and from hunter-gatherer women.

Questions, questions

- Did the Scottish hunter-gatherers invent farming by themselves, or was it brought to Scotland by the Spanish settlers?
- Where did the farmers' sheep and cattle come from? Who tamed them?
- How did farmers get their seeds? It's possible that they were brought long-distance by settlers or traders.
- Why did farming take so long to spread through Scotland? Farming and hunter-gathering lifestyles continued side by side for over 1,000 years.

We still don't know for sure!

4500–3000 BC

Soon after the Spanish settlers arrive, there is a lifestyle revolution in Scotland. For the first time ever, Scottish people begin to settle in one place to live. They raise sheep and cattle, chop down or set fire to trees to clear fields, and plant grain (mostly barley). Whole villages learn to work together, to dig fields and harvest crops. The strongest, cleverest men become chieftains, and organise the teamwork.

Scotland's first farmers have new technology to help them: polished stone axes bound to wooden handles, and stone hoes (blades on sticks for weeding crops and scraping soil). The oldest hoes found so far in Scotland come from Shetland, and were last used around 3400 BC.

As well as hacking their way through prickly brambles and gorse bushes to clear land for growing crops, farmers also weave wicker fences to surround their fields or heap up rough stones to make walls. The fences eventually rot away, but some walls are still standing more than 5,000 years later.

Farmers need homes close to their fields, so they build Scotland's first permanent houses. The trees which are chopped down to clear fields are ideal building material.

Balbridie Hall in Aberdeenshire can sleep 50 people. Built from wood in around 3800 BC, it is 26 metres long and 13 metres wide. No other Scottish timber building will equal its size for almost 4,000 years!

Elsewhere in Scotland, on windswept, almost treeless islands, farmers build whole villages entirely from stone. The village of Skara Brae in Orkney contains ten houses clustered close together, linked by underground sewers. Even the beds are made from solid slabs of rock. Families move in around 3100 BC – about 500 years before the Egyptians build their first pyramid! Nearby, farmers at the Barnhouse Settlement are building what is possibly Scotland's earliest village hall.

The houses of Skara Brae have built-in dressers where farmers keep precious possessions such as pottery bowls. But the farmers are canny (Scots for 'careful').

Stone houses at Skara Brae

What a big carry-oot the boys had brought back.

They also have secret safes under their house floors, to hide their most valuable treasures – or perhaps live fish-bait stored in fresh water.

3000–2500 BC
The farming communities grow rich. They have time to spare – because farming takes up less time than hunting and gathering – and they have leaders who can plan and manage big projects. They build magnificent monuments – standing stones and stone circles, chamber tombs, barrows and cairns. They also carve mysterious patterns on stones and rock balls.

Barrows are huge heaps of earth; cairns are pyramid-shaped piles of stones with hollow spaces inside. Chamber tombs are small stone 'rooms' where the bones of important people are neatly bundled together and laid to rest. The bones are stripped clean first; the dead bodies may be cremated, or butchered, or left out in the open to rot, or birds of prey may eat the flesh. Sometimes, a chief's bones are buried at different places all round the edge of his people's land: perhaps to show who owns it, or perhaps to help protect it.

The Ring of Brodgar, built in Orkney around 2500 BC, measures a vast 104 metres in diameter. It is composed of 60 monoliths (tall single stones) standing in a circle. A project this big probably takes about 80,000 man-hours to complete. Stones are split using wooden wedges hammered into natural cracks in the rock, and moved using wooden rollers.

Haunted?

Centuries later, Scottish people claimed that the standing stones were Stone-Age gods or ancient giants 'frozen' by Christian missionaries. They believed that stone circles were evil – and haunted.

In the 19th and 20th centuries, scholars, tourists and New Age mystics flocked to Scotland to visit the ancient stone monuments. The visitors annoyed one Orkney farmer so much that he smashed one of the famous Stones of Stenness. Soon after, his house mysteriously caught fire – twice!

Frozen out? The Stone-Age gods or ancient giants at the Ring of Brodgar.

The Tomb of the Eagles, on South Ronaldsay Island, is used for 800 years from around 3100 BC by members of the same farming community, who want to rest in peace together with their ancestors. Over 1,600 human bones are buried there, together with about 600 bones from majestic sea-eagles.

Maes Howe tomb, built around 2700 BC on Orkney, is buried under a cairn and entered through a long stone passage. Just once a year, at the winter solstice, the sun shines through the passage and lights up the burial chamber in the centre of the cairn. Why? Even now, no-one is entirely certain, but sunlight on the darkest day might be a symbol of life and rebirth.

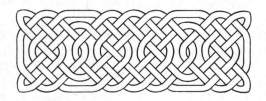

Or have we got it all wrong?

Archaeology has never been easy! Until recently, investigators thought that animal bones found in Scottish burial cairns had been placed there by Stone Age people as offerings to the spirits of the dead. But then they built a replica cairn as an experiment. To their surprise, they found a dead rabbit inside it one morning, dragged there by a pet cat. This made the archaeologists think – perhaps the 'offerings' in ancient cairns had been put there by animals too!

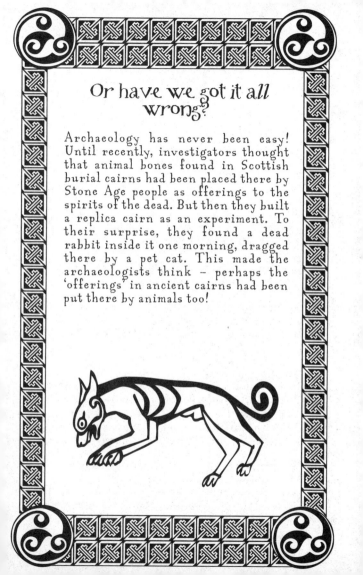

Bronze-Age recipes
WARNING: DO NOT TRY THESE RECIPES TODAY!

Dried Sillocks (baby fish)
1 Remove the fish guts.
2 Wash the fish in salty water.
3 Hang them up out of doors.
4 Eat them when they are completely hard and dry. No cooking needed.[1]

Seaweed
1 Eat raw – it's chewy and crunchy.[2]
   OR
2 Toast on a hot stone[3] by the fire until crisp.

Jelly
1 Find a piece of horn from a young deer.[4]
2 Boil it in water for several hours.
3 Remove the horn and leave the water to cool. It will set, like a jelly.

Burston – Scotland's first toasted cereal?
1 Heat a flat stone[5] in the fire until very hot.
2 Spread a handful of barley-meal over it.
3 Toast the meal until golden.
4 Eat with milk or buttermilk (the liquid left behind after butter has been made).

DO NOT TRY THIS AT HOME!
1, 2. Do not eat uncooked fish or seaweed. Seas and beaches today may be polluted.
3, 5. Do not try this. Some stones explode when heated.
4. Animal horns can carry dangerous diseases – and you would be breaking the law.

CHAPTER TWO

THE BRONZE AGE

c.2500–750 BC

nother revolution reaches Scotland. This time, it's new technology. For the first time, metals are smelted here – the start of a tradition that will last for over 4,000 years.

2500–1000 BC

Land-hungry warrior-chieftains, either from the Netherlands or perhaps from the Alps, arrive over the centuries. They bring new treasures with them – bronze, and beaker-shaped pottery – and slowly take control of many farming communities.

Bronze

Bronze is a metal alloy, a mixture of copper (which is found in Scotland) and tin (which is not). It can be melted and poured into moulds to make beautiful jewellery and new, sharp weapons: axes, knives and Scotland's very first swords. Traders in boats brought tin to Scotland from Cornwall or Spain; expert metal-craftsmen arrived, maybe from continental Europe, maybe from further south in the British Isles. The craftsmen were so skilful that bronze was known in Scotland as 'the work of the gods'.

The newcomers are rich, warlike, and proud of themselves and their possessions. We know this because Bronze-Age burials typically contain just one person, laid all alone in a pit or a stone cist (chest) and surrounded by valuable goods for use – or display – in the next world.

The Migdale Hoard, found in Sutherland, contains bronze axes, a bronze bead necklace, bronze bracelets and anklets, bronze earrings

and bronze bosses (centre-plates for shields), all buried around 2200 BC. Other Bronze-Age Scottish burials contain jewellery made with amber (from the Baltic coast) and jet (a black glossy stone from north-east England). Around 1225 BC, one Bronze-Age warrior living in Blair Drummond is even buried with a European-style waggon – the first-known wheeled transport in Scotland.

Not everyone follows these newfangled burial customs. For example, at Cladh Hallan on the isle of South Uist, one family, in around 1600 BC, decides to keep their ancestors close by soaking them in a peat bog, then burying the mummified bodies under the living-room floor. These are Britain's only known prehistoric mummies.

1159 BC
Disaster! The Hekla Volcano in Iceland erupts, belching out steam, ash and poisonous gas. The sound can be heard even in Scotland! The ash and gas cover the sky and block out the sun for 20 years. During this time there are no summers. For many years more, Scotland's weather grows colder, wetter,

wilder, and generally more unsettled. Crops fail and farm animals die. Around half of Scotland's people perish from cold and hunger. The rest have to fight to survive. Some survivors go hunting, to catch furs and skins to trade. They also sell enemy captives as slaves.

The cave of dead children

Around 1100 BC, parents in north-east Scotland built a temple to dead children. Dozens of dead bodies were laid to rest in a cave near Lossiemouth; their heads were displayed on poles at the cave entrance. Bronze-Age treasures were placed nearby, probably as offerings to the children's spirits.

Puzzling little pieces of hollowed-out pigs' bones were dropped at many Bronze Age sites. They turn out to be children's toys! When tied to a piece of string and whirled round the head quickly, they make a loud roaring and buzzing noise, giving them the name 'buzz-bones'.

1000 BC

By now, the weather is milder. Rare coprolites (fossilised human poo!), found in Shetland, show that Scotland's farmers have a healthy diet: whole grains, fish, wild berries and lamb.

On islands further south and around the coast, Scottish people eat foods that will be thought of as luxuries in later centuries: venison (deer meat), oysters, crabs, salmon, wild raspberries...

750 BC

As wars rage between rival chieftains and hostile tribes, peaceful people in Scotland build safe new places to shelter: hillforts, crannogs, brochs and duns.

Hillforts are strongholds on the top of steep hills, and are often surrounded by earth ramparts. The biggest forts (for example, Eildon Hill, near Melrose) can shelter between 3,000 and 6,000 people (a whole tribe of between 600 and 1200 families).

Crannogs are round wooden houses on artificial islands in the middle of lakes or bogs.

Bronze-Age crannog in a lake.

The only way in is along a causeway (raised path) or by boat.

Brochs are tall, round, stone towers without windows. They are status symbols for powerful families, and temporary shelters in wartime. The Broch of Mousa, in Shetland, built around 100 BC, is over 13 metres tall.

Duns are walled or fenced enclosures in places that are naturally well defended, such as clifftops. The builders sometimes heap up stones to make a wall, then make a fierce fire on either side; the heat fuses the stones together and makes the wall much stronger.

Traders, and a few more warrior chiefs, who come to settle in Scotland, bring new words, ideas and beliefs from mainland Europe. Scottish people now share in a Europe-wide 'Celtic' culture, and speak Celtic languages.

Some rich Celts also share a taste for European delicacies. Pottery jars that once held wine and olives imported from sunny Mediterranean lands have been found as far north as Orkney.

Who were the Celts?

The Celts were people who lived in many different parts of Europe and who all followed a similar way of life. They were not (as is often claimed) an ethnic group or 'race'. Recent DNA research has shown that Celtic peoples – in Scotland and elsewhere in Europe – had several different sets of ancestors.

Celtic peoples had several different sets of ancestors.

Donald thought he'd been kilt!

CHAPTER THREE

THE IRON AGE
750-100 BC

A round 750 BC, another important new technology arrives in Scotland from Celtic Europe: iron-making. Iron is harder, tougher, and more dangerous than bronze. It also makes deadlier weapons. Warriors equipped with the latest iron weapons have a big advantage over their enemies – and great power and prestige.

Celtic warriors also ride fast war-chariots into battle. The oldest-known remains of a Scottish chariot have been found at Newbridge, near Edinburgh. They date from around 400 BC.

The Celts honour warriors, but spend most of their time as farmers. They build farmhouses, byres (cattle-sheds) and grain-stores, surrounded by strong, fenced enclosures. In Scotland, all these buildings are round!

Where trees grow to provide timber, roundhouses have wooden walls and thatched roofs. The biggest and best, like those belonging to rich Aberdeenshire farmers, can be 20 metres in diameter; in Perthshire, they add grand stone gateways.

If possible, farmers nail an enemy's head – or a horse's head – over their door, to bring good luck. The Celts are head-hunters; they believe that each creature's spirit lives in its skull.

In treeless places, like the Hebrides Islands, farmers use turf and stone to build wheelhouses (round houses, with internal walls like the spokes of a wheel) and smaller shelters shaped like a figure-8.

'What this house really needs is an enemy's head above the door!'

100 BC

Scotland's first industrial 'city' grows at Inverness. As well as huge roundhouses for citizens and their chief, there are furnaces, foundries and smithies where iron and bronze are produced then shaped into tools, jewellery and weapons. There are workshops for glassmakers and enamellers, too. Some of the city's output is shipped overseas, as trade. Production continues until at least AD 300.

Further north, enterprising traders take foxes and badgers from the Scottish mainland to Orkney. Their plan? To let the beasties breed, then catch them, kill them and skin them! This is Scotland's first fur farm. Rich islanders enjoy wearing clothes trimmed with badger. The tradition continues for 2,000 years. Until the 20th century, real badger faces were used to trim sporrans.

The Celtic year

Celtic farmers marked the seasons of the farming year with four festivals:

Beltane (1 May)
celebrating warmth, light and life

Lughnasad, pronounced 'Loonahsah'
(1 August), harvest time

Samhain, pronounced 'Savann' (1 November)
a festival of winter, death and darkness

Imbolc (1 February), a springtime festival

These dates remained important for over 2,000 years. They all became Christian festivals, and eventually marked the Quarter Days – the days on which bills were paid, law-court cases were settled and new business ventures begun. Some – especially Samhain (All Saints' Day) – are still celebrated today, although their original meaning has been forgotten.

CHAPTER FOUR

ROMAN SCOTLAND

AD 55–211

To most other peoples in Europe at this time, Scotland is a shadowy, mysterious land, right at the edge of the world. The first armies from Rome land in Britain in 55 BC. They sail away, and do not venture into Scotland – yet.

AD 43–79
Roman armies invade and conquer the southern British Isles, and get to hear about the Celtic tribes in Scotland. For the first time, we have written evidence about Scotland – but it is produced by Roman writers, and this leads to problems for future historians.

The Romans think that the Celts are barbarians and savages, so they ignore many Celtic achievements, such as brilliant metalwork and glass-making. Instead, they tell how Celts rush naked into battle, protected only by war-paint and 'magic' torcs (necklaces). They describe how Celtic men and women love big jewellery, have long, wild, flowing hair, and wear bright, striped and checked clothes. They are shocked by tall, strong Celtic women with hot tempers and loud voices, and by druids (Celtic priests and scholars) who make human sacrifices in silent, sinister, blood-spattered sacred groves.

The Celtic tribes are fiercely independent. There is no united Scottish nation. People in different parts of Scotland have their own separate versions of Celtic culture. They even speak different – but related – languages.

We know the names of the different tribes in Scotland because the Romans list them, but we don't know whether the names are quite right. The Romans probably got them second or third hand, passed on from Scotland by conquered – or friendly – south British tribes.

Celtic tribes in Roman Scotland

AD 79

Agricola, the Roman governor of Britain, sends spy-ships to sail all round the Scottish coast. The Romans want to find out more about this unknown land. They discover that the narrowest part of Scotland, between the River Forth and the River Clyde, is very wet and boggy. The Romans wonder: is the northern part of Scotland really an island?

Roman armies advance into Scotland, keeping east of the Grampian mountains on the west. Their plan is to block the entrance to each glen (narrow valley) leading to the Celtic tribes' homelands. They build camps as temporary shelters, and strong forts for longer stays.

The greatest Roman fort (at Inchtuthil, near Perth) has 64 barrack blocks, 4 officers' houses, a hospital, six grain-stores, a drill-hall, a workshop and a headquarters building. It takes about 2.7 million man-hours to construct – that means about 1,000 men working full-time for a year.

Roman forts and Roman nails

The fort at Inchtuthil was abandoned by the Romans in AD 86-87, as it was too difficult to guard and keep supplied amidst hostile territory. Since then, over a million Roman iron nails have been found at the site. Many have been sold to Christian groups all around the world – because they are from around the same date as the nails with which Jesus Christ was crucified.

AD 84

The separate tribes in Scotland have never before been threatened by a common enemy. Now they come face to face with the Romans at the Battle of Mons Graupius (Grampian Mountains), in Aberdeenshire. The Romans have stronger, longer swords, and are better organised. Roman writers record that 30,000 Celtic tribesmen die, and that Celtic warriors set fire to their own homes, and even kill their own wives and children, to stop them falling into Roman hands.

The Celts speak

The Roman historian Tacitus recorded the earliest-known words spoken by anyone from Scotland. The speaker was Calgacus ('Swordsman'), chief of the Caledonii tribe.

Looking at the destruction caused by the Roman invasion, Calgacus remarked, 'They make a desert, and call it peace.'

AD 86–105
Having watched the Celts destroy their own farms and homes, the Romans realise they will not be able to find food and shelter for themselves, so they have to retreat.

AD 108
The Ninth Legion of the Roman Army marches out from Eboracum (now York, in England) – and completely disappears! Some say that its 5,000 men are slaughtered in Scotland.

AD 122

The Romans build Hadrian's Wall (just south of today's Scottish–English border) to keep out raiders from Scotland. It stretches for 117 km, between the River Tyne in the east and the River Solway in the west.

Hadrian's Wall is the largest building project undertaken in the British Isles so far. It contains almost 750,000 cubic tonnes of rock, which takes seven years to transport to the site from nearby quarries, using around 1,000 ox-carts and over 2,000 pack-horses and mules. When completed, the wall is painted white and marked with vertical red lines to give the impression of neatly trimmed blocks of stone.

Romans guarding Hadrian's Wall do not think much of the Celtic tribes who attack them. In a letter home, found at the Roman fort of Vindolanda, one soldier calls them *Brittunculi* (miserable little Brits).

AD 139–143

The Romans advance into Scotland again, and build a second barrier, the Antonine Wall, across the Lowlands, from the River Clyde to the River Forth.

Marcus plans to write home for warm socks and underpants.

The wall is made of slabs of turf piled on a rock foundation; it stretches for 60 km and is 2.75 metres high. A wooden walkway runs along the top, for lookouts to patrol.

The north side of the Antonine Wall is protected by a huge ditch, 12 metres wide and 3.7 metres deep. This is filled with *lilia* (lilies) – the grimly humorous Roman name for pits filled with deadly, sharpened, wooden stakes hidden under bracken and heather.

The world comes to Scotland!

Roman Scotland was a multicultural place:

Lollius Urbicus, the Roman governor in charge of building the Antonine Wall, was from Algeria. His workmen included soldiers from the Balkans and the north of Italy. Scouts sent ahead of Roman troops to spy out the land came from Spain.

Thousands more Roman soldiers lived in forts along Hadrian's Wall. They had been recruited from many different parts of the Roman empire: Germany, the Netherlands, France, Bulgaria, Hungary, Syria and North Africa.

Traders from Roman lands also visited and settled south of the wall.

By law, Roman soldiers were forbidden to marry while on active service. But many fell in love with women from south Scottish tribes, and had half-Scottish children.

AD 161–163
The Antonine Wall proves impossible to defend or to keep supplied with food and fuel – the Romans abandon it after only 20 years.

AD 180 and AD 197
Several times, tribes from Scotland surge across Hadrian's Wall to attack the Romans. For a while, the Romans begin to flee, but eventually they 'buy' peace by offering treasure to the attackers.

AD 208
Led by Emperor Septimius Severus, Roman armies advance north of the ruined Antonine Wall, hoping to exterminate the attacking tribes. At first they appear to be succeeding, but in 211 the emperor dies and, without a leader, they retreat again.

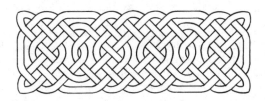

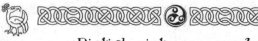

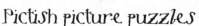

Pictish picture puzzles

For hundreds of years, historians have puzzled over stone carvings left by the Pictish people. Most date from the time when the Pictish kingdom was the most powerful in Scotland, between around AD 400 and 800. Some carvings are scratched on the surface of boulders. Possibly, they mark boundaries or holy places. Others are carefully arranged on tall standing stones. Why? Historians think that many carved standing stones are tombstones or memorials, honouring powerful people. Other standing stones may mark meeting places, where Christian missionaries stood to preach. Historians have now learned to 'read' the picture-symbol code.

Baffling balls

Before the Picts created picture-stones, they also carved mysterious stone balls. Each one is about the size of a large orange, and is decorated with raised knobs or incised (cut) grooves and spirals. Over 300 balls have been found so far in the lands where the Picts lived. They are all beautifully crafted, and must have taken weeks to make. What were they for? No-one knows for certain. Possibly they were oracles, used to foretell the future. Perhaps they were passed from speaker to speaker at Pictish tribal meetings. Or maybe they were thrown or bowled for sport...

CHAPTER five

PICTS AND SCOTS

AD 297–410

I n AD 297, the roman poet Eumenius makes a speech praising Roman victories. He mentions a tribe whose name has not been written down until now – the *Picti*, of north-east Scotland.

Who were the Picts? People have suggested all kinds of outlandish possibilities, from Phoenicians (members of an ancient east-Mediterranean civilisation), to mysterious tribes from the Holy Land, or the inhabitants of secret underground tunnels. It has even been suggested that they were exiles from Atlantis – a fantasy continent said to have disappeared beneath the Atlantic Ocean.

Today, historians think that the Picts were the descendants of the Celtic tribes who fought the Romans at the battle of Mons Graupius in AD 84. Their Roman name, *Picti*, means 'Painted People', and is probably related to *pryd*, a Celtic word meaning 'shape' or 'pattern'. Both words tell us that the Picts painted or tattooed themselves with magical protective designs.

AD 342–343 and AD 360

Romans in Britain are attacked by pirates from Ireland who raid Roman ships and plunder villages on the coast. The Romans called these pirates *Scoti* (Scots). This was probably their version of a Celtic word *sgud*, which means 'sail'.

AD 367–368

The Picts and the Scots launch a joint attack on Roman Britain, capturing and killing important Romano-British leaders.

AD 369

The Romans strengthen Hadrian's Wall one more time.

Scots – from Ireland?

Yes, that's what the Romans said. But to people in Roman times the lands on both sides of the Irish Sea were one single region. Later, the places where they lived – now known as west Scotland and Northern Ireland – were given separate names. (See map on next page.)

The Scots (or Gaels) belonged to several different Celtic tribes, but shared similar lifestyles. They spoke a Celtic language, like the Picts' but slightly different; this language was the ancestor of today's Scottish and Irish Gaelic. They travelled throughout their home region, to trade and fight and sometimes to marry.

At the narrowest point, it was only 19 km (12 miles) from one side of the Irish Sea to the other, and it was much easier to hop into a boat and row or sail across the sea than it was to struggle up and down steep mountains or across wild, boggy moors, trying to travel eastwards through Scotland.

Scots live on both sides of the Irish Sea.

c. AD 370

Around this time, a Celtic chieftain commanding the hillfort at Traprain Law, near Edinburgh, buries a splendid collection of Roman silver coins, cups and jewellery. It's possible that this was a bribe, paid by the Romans, to stop tribes from Scotland attacking them.

AD 382

Roman army leader Magnus Maximus gives help to the Celtic tribes of southern Scotland. He hopes that they will join him to fight against the Picts and the Scots.

AD 410

Roman rule in the British Isles comes to an end, due to political quarrels among rival leaders of the Roman empire. The Romans abandon Hadrian's Wall.

Celtic tribes close to the Wall seize their opportunity. They carry away stone from the wall and from Roman forts to use for their own construction projects, and take over abandoned Roman buildings.

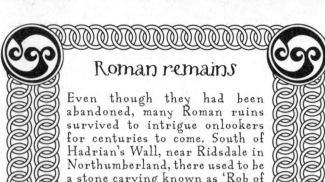

Roman remains

Even though they had been abandoned, many Roman ruins survived to intrigue onlookers for centuries to come. South of Hadrian's Wall, near Ridsdale in Northumberland, there used to be a stone carving known as 'Rob of Risingham'. Today, historians think that 'Rob' was actually a woman – the Roman goddess Diana. Now, only the figure's legs remain – the rest of the carving was destroyed in the 18th century by a local landowner who didn't want tourists visiting his land.

Rob of
Risingham

CHAPTER SIX

FOUR KINGDOMS

AD 410–843

cotland is now free from the threat of further Roman invasion, but the land is still divided among many different tribes. Slowly, they are united by warlike leaders to create four large, powerful kingdoms and several smaller, weaker, ones.

The four main groups are:

- The Picts
- The Scots
- The Britons
- The Angles

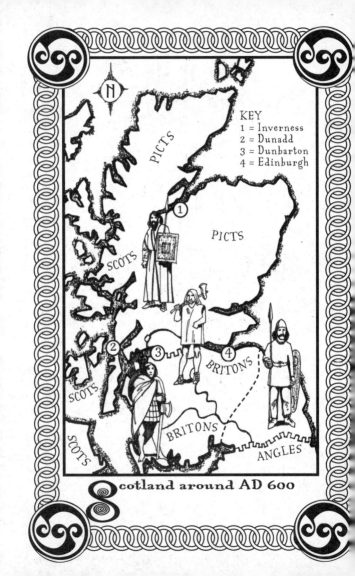

KEY
1 = Inverness
2 = Dunadd
3 = Dunbarton
4 = Edinburgh

PICTS

PICTS

SCOTS

SCOTS

SCOTS

BRITONS

BRITONS

ANGLES

Scotland around AD 600

Pictland is in the north and north-west of Scotland. The capital is probably near modern Inverness.

The Scots rule the kingdom of Dál Riata, comprising south-west Scotland and part of north-eastern Ireland. The capital is Dunadd, near modern Kilmartin in Argyll.

The Britons rule several smaller kingdoms: Strathclyde (around Alt Clut – modern Dumbarton); Gododdin (around Dun Eidin – modern Edinburgh); and Rheged (either side of the Solway Firth).

The Angles hold Northumbria, from around Whitby in Yorkshire to north of the River Tweed.

There is no fixed border between Scotland and England, as those two nations do not yet exist. (The dotted line on the map shows the modern border.) One 'Scottish' kingdom (Rheged) includes part of what is now England, and one 'English' kingdom (Northumbria) includes part of modern Scotland.

Kingdoms grow bigger or smaller, depending on the power of each king and the strength of his army. Local chiefs and warriors decide which king to follow; their choices can keep a king on his throne or remove him from power.

The peoples of Scotland speak four different languages. Communications are not easy…

The Picts speak a language that scholars call P-Celtic – similar to modern Welsh.

The Scots speak Q-Celtic – similar to modern Scottish and Irish Gaelic.

The Britons speak P-Celtic, but a different dialect from the Picts.

The Angles speak Anglo-Saxon – related to modern Dutch and German, and the ancestor of modern English.

The Picts

- Were descended from Celtic tribes in north and east Scotland.

- Had the largest kingdom, with the most people.

- Carved portraits of themselves, magic patterns, and symbols of power – especially bulls – on hundreds of rocks and tall stone slabs throughout their kingdom.

- Wrote using a script called Ogham, made of patterns of straight lines.

- Had a navy. They attacked Orkney in AD 681.

- Left clues to where they lived in place-names beginning 'Pet' or 'Pit' (piece of land) or 'Aber' (river mouth).

- Were at their strongest between AD 685 and 820.

- Lost all their leaders in a Viking attack in AD 839.

- United with the Scots or Gaels to form a new kingdom (later known as Alba) in AD 843.

The Scots

- Were descended from Celtic tribes living on both sides of the Irish Sea.

- Were strong enough to demand treasure and slaves from Irish kings.

- Traded with Wales, Cornwall, Ireland and France.

- Made intricate and impressive metalwork.

- Wrote using Ogham script.

- Left clues to where they lived in place-names beginning 'Bal' (village or farm) and 'Dun' (fort).

- Were conquered by the Picts in AD 740.

- Were attacked by Vikings from AD 792 or 793.

- United with the Picts in AD 843 to form the kingdom later known as Alba.

The Britons

- Were descended from Celtic tribes living on both sides of Hadrian's wall.

- Copied Roman customs.

- Had trading links with other British tribes further south.

- Imported wine and spices from France, and glasses from Germany.

- Left clues to where they lived in place names such as 'Linn' (waterfall) and 'gow' (hollow – as in 'Glasgow').

- Their eastern fort, Edinburgh, was conquered by the Angles in AD 638. Stirling became their new power-base.

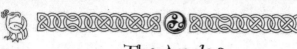

The Angles

- Were descended from settlers who arrived from north Germany.

- Built grand royal halls, made of wood, for their kings.

- Made amazing gold and garnet decorations for weapons and armour.

- Left clues to where they lived in place names ending with 'ham' or 'tun' (village).

- Invaded northwards, but were stopped by Picts at the battle of Dunnichen Moss near Forfar in AD 685.

- Became part of Alba (the new kingdom of Scotland) in AD 973.

Kings and warriors

Kings live on top of volcanoes! The chief royal forts of the Britons, at Alt Clut (Dumbarton Rock) and Castle Rock in Edinburgh, are built on top of huge plugs of solidified lava left by long-dead volcanoes. So is Dunadd, the most important stronghold in Dál Riata. Their steep, sheer sides are very difficult for enemies to climb. For the same reason, Bamburgh fort, belonging to the Anglian kings, is perched on a tall cliff by the sea.

We know the names of a few rulers, though others remain a mystery. Domnall Brecc ('Spotty Donald'), a Scot, rules Kintyre from AD 629 to AD 642 – and is remembered for all the wrong reasons. He fights four big battles against Ulster (a kingdom in the north-east of Ireland), and loses them all.

More successful is the Pictish king Oengus mac Fergusa (Angus son of Fergus), who defeats many rivals to become king of Pictland, forcing his most important enemy to become a monk. He conquers Dál Riata around AD 741.

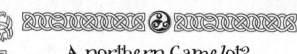

A northern Camelot?

Did King Arthur, famous leader of the Knights of the Round Table, live in Edinburgh? Some poets and bards claim that he was high king among the Britons, and that the mountain in Edinburgh, still called 'Arthur's Seat' to this day, was a meeting place for his followers.

It's a hard life being royal. Kings have many, many duties. Some are pleasant, some are dangerous. Some are magical! If you were king, you'd be expected to:

• **Defend your land and conquer new territory. There are wars, wars, wars...**
So many kings die fighting – and the future of a nation can depend on a single battle. In AD 685, King Bridei, ruler of the Picts, leads his men against the mighty Anglian army. If he loses, all of north and east Scotland will be ruled by the Angles, and will have to speak the Anglo-Saxon language and obey Anglian laws. Scotland, as a separate nation, will never come into existence...

• **Marry a wife from a rival kingdom**
This sounds like a good way of making friends and bringing peace, but all too often it leads to quarrels. Close family members find themselves fighting on different sides. And when a king dies, there are many heirs – brothers, uncles, in-laws, stepchildren, cousins – each with a family claim to inherit his throne.

• Take part in magic rituals

Kings are links between gods and humans, and it's their task to bring wealth, strength and fertility to their lands. In Dál Riata, kings climb to the top of the fort at Dunadd, where there are magic royal symbols – a bowl, a throne, and a hole shaped like a footprint – carved into the rock face. In a grand gesture, the king fits his foot into the hole as a sign that he is master of the kingdom.

The footprint stone at Dunadd

Giant strides

Some legends claim that the Dunadd footprint was left there by the ancient Celtic hero Ossian, as he stomped across Scotland's mountain-tops.

Others tell how Irish hero Finn MacCool walked from Ireland to Scotland across the Giant's Causeway (a huge slab of solidified lava, cracked into 4,000 columns, that once stretched between Ireland and western Scotland). But an enormous Scottish giant – much, much, bigger than Finn – came to greet him. Finn was so frightened that he ran back to Ireland, pulling up the causeway behind him and hurling it away! That is why only some of it can still be seen – the rest is under the sea.

Attack of the 195~foot woman

Later, around AD 900, chroniclers (early historians) on both sides of the Irish Sea reported that a drowned giant woman had been washed ashore in Scotland. She was 195 feet (59.5 metres) tall, with a body 'as white as a swan', and her hair was 18 feet (5.5 metres) long.

• Host wonderful parties

Kings give lavish feasts, with mead (honey wine), meat, music and storytelling. In return for this royal generosity, warriors are expected to fight and die for their king.

• Hand out treasure

Stone moulds at Dunadd are used for casting precious metals to make beautiful brooches – as round as the moon and with a long pin, like a spear. The kings of Dál Riata give these to loyal warriors as a rich reward and a badge of honour. The bigger the brooch, the better, braver – and probably more boastful – the warrior!

• Keep soothsayers and bards at court

These secretaries and spin-doctors remember traditional laws and pass on royal family history. They also invent myths to explain their king's right to rule – and may even try a bit of forgery.

For example, soon after AD 900, royal poets add a few lines to an ancient list of kings. They are trying to claim that the ruling family of Dál Riata is descended from a famous Irish hero. But the new words are slightly different from the rest of the text; ways of speaking and writing have changed over time. The forgery is eventually discovered – but not for over 1,000 years!

• Keep moving

Kings travel all round their kingdoms, to show who's boss, check up on what's happening, and collect taxes. It's an honour to receive a royal visit from a king and his warriors, but it's horribly expensive to feed and entertain them!

• Make lists

A few kings get scribes (professional writers) to write down lists of what their people owe them in taxes – an exciting new idea that is sure to catch on! Around AD 650, the Senchus Fer nAlban (History of the Scots) is written in Dál Riata. In spite of its title, it's not a history book, but the oldest-known list of taxpayers from any British kingdom.

Daily life in the four kingdoms

c.AD 500–700
There are no towns in Scotland yet, though there are many in England and Europe. Most ordinary families in Scotland live on farms (either their own, or a richer landlord's). They grow food, try to keep warm and dry, and pay taxes – usually in the form of cattle.

Country life is not easy. A change in climate brings colder, wetter weather. Houses are made of wood, wattle-and-daub (woven twigs covered with mud or clay and animal hair) or turf, so it's hard to keep them weatherproof. The latest homes are built to new designs copied from the Anglians. They are no longer round, in the traditional Celtic style, but square or rectangular with corners.

The growing season – the time when crops flourish and ripen – is now a whole month shorter than before, and fierce, hungry wild animals, especially wolves, attack sheep and cattle. Among the people, natural population increase means that there is less land to go round.

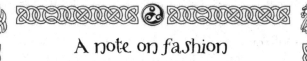

A note on fashion

To keep warm, everyone in Scotland wears the same kinds of clothes: cloaks, tunics and long trousers, just like the Pictish warrior portrayed on the famous Rhynie stone, carved around AD 700. Tunics are short for men and below the knee for women; trousers are for men only. Men and women grow their hair long, and may dye or bleach it.

Everyone wears jewellery and face paint – even monks! At this point, no-one is wearing kilts or tartan; these are later inventions. But, in cold weather, people in Scotland do wear some of Europe's first hoodies. Thick woollen cloaks with hoods from Celtic Britain have been popular since Roman times. A splendid hooded cape, decorated with fancy fringes, was lost in an Orkney bog around AD 400, where it survived to be discovered in the 20th century.

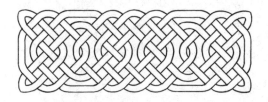

Villagers divide their farmland into strips and share it out by lottery. That way, each family gets a turn at farming some productive land, or 'inbye', and a share of the poor, rough land, or 'outbye'.

In summertime, farmers lead their cattle up to high mountain pastures, or across wild, windswept moors. For a few short months, there will be grass growing there to feed them. The farmers live in shielings (temporary shelters). They milk the cows and make butter and cheese to store for winter. The rest of their food is plain and simple: grains, wild berries, wild deer, fish and shellfish (if they are lucky enough to catch them).

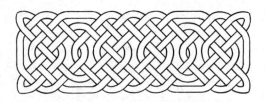

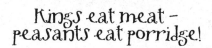

Kings eat meat –
peasants eat porridge!

Scotland's favourite traditional food is a sloppy, sticky, gritty, greyish sludge called porridge. It's made by soaking oatmeal (ground or crushed oats) in water for hours, then boiling the mixture, while stirring it all the time. The stirring should always be clockwise – in the same way that the sun seems to circle the earth. Porridge experts don't say what might happen if you stir in the opposite direction, but the porridge would probably go lumpy. The water should come from a pure mountain spring, but that is not always possible. Traditionally, porridge is served hot, either all by itself or with a sprinkling of salt. It should be thick enough to cling to 'the inside of your ribs'.

Oatmeal porridge sounds as if it should be a very ancient food, eaten by Stone-Age people, but in fact it is a fairly new arrival, because oats were not introduced to Scotland from mainland Europe until about AD 600. Archaeologists have found traces of some of the first oats to grow in Britain near Dunadd in Dál Riata.

An earlier kind of porridge, made of whole barley grains stewed with milk, was eaten by islanders in the Outer Hebrides. Their cooking pots have been found by archaeologists – with microscopic pieces of porridge still sticking to them after 2,500 years!

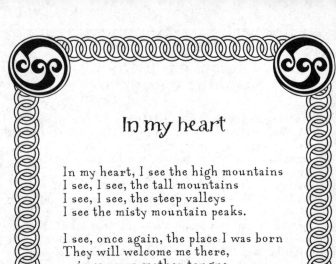

In my heart

In my heart, I see the high mountains
I see, I see, the tall mountains
I see, I see, the steep valleys
I see the misty mountain peaks.

I see, once again, the place I was born
They will welcome me there,
   in my own mother tongue
There I will find love and kindness
Priceless treasures.

In my heart, I see the high mountains
I see, I see, the tall mountains
I see, I see, the steep valleys
I see the misty mountain peaks.

*Translated from the original
Gaelic words composed in 1865
by John Cameron of Ballachulish.*

Chapter Seven

OLD BELIEFS, NEW IDEAS

c.AD 500-800

Around the year 500, the first Christian missionaries arrive in Scotland, from Ireland and Northumbria – and come face to face with druids (Celtic holy men). Druids are doctors, poets, priests, historians, magicians and fortune-tellers. They spend 12 long years studying the secret knowledge of their kingdom and remembering it precisely. They say prayers, make sacrifices, give advice – and utter dire warnings.

Celtic peoples – Picts, Scots and Britons – are very superstitious. They protect themselves with lucky numbers (three and seven), lucky birds (wrens – it's considered lucky to kill them!), lucky trees (rowan – which keeps witches away), and lucky plants – especially oak (so tall, so strong!) and mistletoe (poisonous and deadly, it is sacred to the Moon). Led by druids, the Celts make offerings of their most precious treasures and people, by throwing them into watery places such as lakes or bogs. They kill their sacrifices before they throw them in; swords are 'killed' by bending them.

For the Celts, Scotland is an enchanted land, full of ghosts and spirits. They think they see floating islands, and hollow hills where the *sidhe* (pronounced 'shee'), or fairies, live. They dream of visiting Tir Nan Og (the Land of the Young) beneath the waves. They honour their ancestors and worship giant, man-eating gods with horns on their heads and three faces. They believe in magic, and monsters!

Beware! Celtic monsters!

- **Kelpies:** fierce, flesh-eating water horses who gallop out of the waves.
- **Banshees:** wailing spirit-women who foretell death and disaster.
- **The Morrigan:** a bloodstained, shapeshifting carrion crow that devours dead bodies on the battlefield.

- **The Cailleach Bheur** (pronounced Cally Vaar): a grim old crone who freezes the life out of everything.
- **Selkies:** seal-women (and occasionally men) who break human hearts.
- **Mermen of the Minch:** like mermaids, but male – and blue!
- **Hounds of Hell:** white dogs with red ears. They race across the night sky, chasing victims to their doom.
- **Morag:** a friendly creature living in Loch Morar, Scotland's deepest lake.
- **Glastaigs:** kindly green women (sometimes half-woman, half-goat) who watch over children and farm animals.

Last, but by no means least...

- **The Loch Ness Monster!** Is she a snake? Is she a whale? Is she a dinosaur, surviving from 60 million years ago? Or is she just a pattern of waves, raised by wild winds blowing across the water?

  The first recorded sighting of 'Nessie' was in AD 565. Today, she is one of Scotland's top tourist attractions – whether she exists or not!

  ?

AD 550–700
Christian missionaries get busy in Scotland.

• **St Ninian** (a Briton; dies around AD 550)
Some say he built a famous 'White Church' –
the first in south-west Scotland. Others say he
went to find 'lost' Christians whose families
had been living there since Roman times.

• **St Kentigern** (a Pict; dies around AD 620)
Also called St Mungo (Dear One), he founds
a church at Glasgow. Today, Glasgow
Cathedral stands on the site.

• **St Oran** (a Scot; dies around AD 575)
Oran lives on a lonely island. He decides to be
bricked up alive inside his new church, as a
sacrifice to God.

• **St Aidan** (a Scot; dies around AD 651)
He travels to the Anglian kingdom of
Northumbria, where he founds a famous
monastery at Lindisfarne, on Holy Island.

Saints across the sea

The two greatest early Celtic saints cross the
Irish Sea – in opposite directions – to live and
work in each other's homelands.

St Patrick (c.AD 387 – AD 461), a Briton from Scotland, goes to Ireland...

- Young Patrick is kidnapped by slave-trading
  Irish pirates from his home in Strathclyde.
- After many years he is freed and travels home
  to Scotland.
- There he has a dream telling him that he must
  go back to Ireland as a Christian missionary.
- He spends the rest of his life in Ireland,
  preaching.
- His followers claim that he performed many
  miracles – some say he drove all the snakes
  out of Ireland!

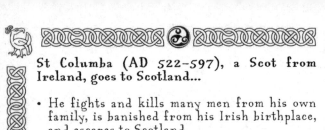

St Columba (AD 522–597), a Scot from Ireland, goes to Scotland...

- He fights and kills many men from his own family, is banished from his Irish birthplace, and escapes to Scotland.
- He changes his name from Crimthann (Wily Fox) to Colomb (Dove of Peace).
- He spends his life travelling through Scotland, spreading Christianity.
- In AD 563 he builds a monastery on the small, bleak, bare, cold, rainy, windswept, isolated island of Iona.
- Amazingly, people hurry to join him there, his preaching is so powerful!
- He is said to talk with angels. Dazzling rays of light flash down from the sky to bless him.
- Locked gates of forts and castles fly open at a sign from his holy cross.
- He dares to challenge wizards at the Pictish royal court – and wins.
- He meets the Loch Ness Monster in AD 565 – and tells it to behave better!
- St Columba's bones become one of Scotland's national treasures. They are placed in a box of real gold and silver (the Monymusk Reliquary) and carried into battle at the head of the Scottish army.
- Pictish kings invent a new name, Malcolm (it means 'Servant of Columba'), to show their respect for him.

AD 600–800

Christianity brings big changes to Scottish learning, law and art. Monks set up libraries, write new books, and make copies of important texts.

• Columba is said to have written 300 books, all by hand!

• Adhomnan, a monk at Iona, writes 'The Law of the Innocent' in AD 697. It is a collection of rules for protecting women, children – and monks – in wartime, and is one of the world's earliest declarations of human rights.

• The monks decorate holy books – such as parts of the Bible or collections of prayers – with glowing, swirling patterns based on traditional Celtic designs. The most famous is the Book of Kells, made at Iona. (It is now in the library of Trinity College, Dublin.)

• Books are written on vellum – cleaned, smoothed calfskin. About 185 calves are killed to complete the Book of Kells alone. But the minerals used to make the monks' coloured paints include lead (for red) and arsenic (for yellow). Both are poisonous, and will make their users very ill, ulcerating their skin and rotting their bones.

• Priests and people pay for tall stone crosses, carved with Christian pictures and Celtic patterns. the crosses mark meeting places for preaching and praying. In Dál Riata they are topped by a wide circle. This is not a religious symbol, but a clever solution to a technical difficulty. The circle supports the long, heavy arms of the cross, which would otherwise drop off!

8th-century
stone cross,
Iona

The cross at Ruthwell, south-west Scotland, was carved by Anglian craftworkers from Northumbria. They covered it with stories from the Bible, told in pictures, and added lines from a religious poem, carved in runes – the oldest-known form of writing in Anglo-Saxon or English.

AD 663

A Synod (meeting of Christian leaders) is held at Whitby, Northumbria. Their task: to solve a problem that mixes maths, politics, faith and fashion. Priests and monks in Scotland and Ireland calculate the date of Easter (the most important Christian festival) in their own unique way. They also tonsure (shave) their hair in a different style from the monks in mainland Europe, and they wear beards. They even paint black rims around their eyes, an ancient Celtic custom.

Should they be made to change and obey Church calendars approved by the Pope in Rome? The answer is yes! The Synod rules that they should change their haircuts, too.

AD 733

A new saint arrives – in pieces – but how? Here are two different stories, both ancient. You can choose which you prefer to believe. No-one knows for sure which is true.

• St Rule is a monk in Greece. One night, he has a dream. It warns him to take some of St Andrew's bones (which are housed nearby) and sail westwards. The dream tells him that wherever his ship reaches land, he should build a monastery. It will become a place of peace where pilgrims can be healed. St Rule sails for days, weeks, months – and then he is shipwrecked. Still clutching the precious bones, he staggers ashore at the little village of Kilrymont, on the east coast of Scotland, and builds his monastery there.

• Bishop Acca, an Angle from Hexham (Northumbria), brings the bones of St Andrew to Scotland. The bones are housed in a monastery on the east coast of Scotland, set up several years earlier by followers of St Columba.

Whichever story is true, the town beside the monastery soon becomes known as St Andrews. A fine cathedral is built there. The holy bones are kept in a huge and splendid container, weighing one-third of a tonne. Pilgrims flock to pray beside it, and some report miracles.

St Andrew was one of Jesus' earliest followers, and was the brother of St Peter, the first Pope. He lived and preached in the Middle East and eastern Europe in the first century AD. He never saw – and probably never heard of – Scotland. But nonetheless he becomes Scotland's patron saint.

Around AD 950, St Andrew's day (30 November) is made a public holiday for all Scotland, celebrated with street games and processions of people carrying garlands of evergreen leaves. The holiday is good fun, but it also has a political purpose. Being protected by St Andrew helps Scots rulers and people to feel independent of England, and closely linked – like brother saints Andrew and Peter – to the very powerful Pope in Rome.

A miraculous saltire appeared in the sky.

A sign in the sky

In AD 735, just two years after St Andrew's bones had reached Scotland, Pictish soldiers fighting against the Angles saw a huge white cross against the bright blue sky. It looked just like the X-shaped cross on which St Andrew had been crucified. The Picts believed the saint was fighting on their side, and won the battle!

Ever since then, the Saltire – a white, X-shaped cross on a deep blue background – has been the national flag of Scotland. Today, it is seen everywhere, from the new Scottish Parliament building to the faces of Scottish football fans.

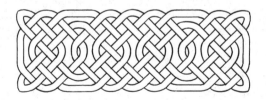

Raiders from the sea, the Vikings have arrived in Scotland – and they decide to stay.

CHAPTER EIGHT

VIKING SCOTLAND

AD 793- c.1100

Scotland is still divided, and often at war. And now a new threat reaches Scottish shores – raiders from the sea. The Vikings have arrived! They sail in fast, sleek longships to attack towns and villages all round the coast of Scotland, killing, plundering and seizing captives to carry away and sell as slaves.

In good weather, with steady winds, the voyage from Norway to Scotland does not take long. The Vikings are expert sailors, and can cross the sea between Norway and Scotland in much less than a week. Their ships are designed to skim over the waves, so sailing is like a wet, windy roller-coaster ride. The decks are open and very crowded, and there is no shelter on board. It's almost impossible to sleep.

AD 793

Vikings attack Lindisfarne, the greatest monastery in the kingdom of the Angles, and a famous centre of art and learning.

Churches and monasteries are the Vikings' favourite targets. They house rich treasures, such as gold and silver crosses, holy books in jewelled covers, and silk altar-cloths. But the Vikings are not art-lovers – or at least, they don't admire Celtic art. They steal these beautiful objects because they can sell them or break them up to re-use the precious materials they contain. One Celtic reliquary (casket for a saint's bones) was found buried in a Viking noblewoman's grave. She had been using it as her jewellery box.

AD 795–826

Vikings raid Scotland's largest and best-known monastery – the one founded by St

Columba on the island of Iona in the Inner Hebrides – over and over again. They kill 68 Iona monks, including the abbot, St Blaithmac. In AD 823, he chooses to be hacked to death while praying, rather than hand over the monastery's holy treasures. The surviving monks flee to Dunkeld, which is further inland and safer from Viking raids.

Where the Vikings landed

Traditional stories tell how Scottish nuns took extreme measures to stop the Vikings assaulting them or capturing them for slavery. In around AD 870, as Viking raiders broke into their nunnery at Coldingham in Berwickshire, the holy sisters cut off their own lips and noses, to present ghastly, bloody faces to their attackers.

Viking warrior style

Rich Vikings wear a coat of mail. It's made of countless rings of iron wire, all carefully linked together. It's very, very expensive, and only top warlords can afford it. Ordinary warriors wear armour made of reindeer hide, which is probably tougher!

Helmets with spikes on top are popular, but costly. Less wealthy warriors wear padded leather caps. Viking warriors don't wear helmets with horns or wings – these are invented by historians and artists in later centuries.

fearsome fighters

Monks and nuns were no match for the ruthless Viking warriors, who were famous throughout Europe for their fighting skills. These included some unusual – and deadly – tricks, such as:

- Throwing spears with both hands at once.
- Catching enemy spears in flight and hurling them back.
- Terrifying their enemies by going berserk – stamping, shouting, wearing magic bearskins, eating poisonous fungi (which made them wild and fearless), chewing their shields in a rage, then stampeding wildly towards terrified enemies.
- Fighting like a wild boar. Warriors charged in a boar-snout (V-shaped) formation called *svinfylking*, with shields overlapping and spears bristling.
- Swinging a mighty two-handed battle-axe in a deadly surprise attack. Axemen could not carry shields since they had no free hand. So they hid in the ranks of ordinary warriors, then suddenly rushed forward.

AD 850

Whole Viking families – as well as warriors –
begin to settle in north and west Scotland, and
in Orkney and Shetland. They bring Viking
words, ideas, beliefs, objects and ways of life
with them.

We know this from the evidence of burials.
Viking graves of men, women and children
have been found in Scotland, dating from
around AD 850. At that time, the Vikings are
still pagans (this was the term Christians used
to describe non-Christians). They are buried
in boats, or boat-shaped stone enclosures,
together with Viking-style weapons, jewellery
and other items that they might need
in the next world.

Scar boat burial

One of the best-preserved, and most puzzling, Viking burials is at Scar, in Orkney. It contains a man, a young child, and a woman aged about 70, all laid to rest in a wooden rowing boat, with valuable goods surrounding them. The woman is extraordinarily old by Viking standards: few Viking people lived for more than 35 years. But who is she, and how did she live so long? Why are the man and child buried with her? Are they members of a family who all died suddenly, or an ancient wise woman and her servants? No-one knows.

Yule

Viking settlers brought their own traditional festivals with them to Scotland, especially Yule. This was celebrated for 12 days – or sometimes a month – at midwinter (around 21 December), with feasting, drinking, songs, stories and jokes. Yule was orignally a festival for the dead, which is why it was held at the darkest, coldest, most lifeless season of the year. It was a time for honouring ancestors, and asking them to send good luck to living family members. It was also a time when dead spirits walked the earth. Viking families always kept an empty place at Yule feasts for ancestor-spirits, and took great care if they ventured outdoors after dark!

Like some later tourists, the newly arrived Vikings can't resist leaving their names on important monuments. The prehistoric tomb at Maes Howe, Orkney (see page 36), has one of the largest collections of Viking runic inscriptions (carved writing) in the world.

English men who meet Vikings complain that they care too much for their appearance. Vikings comb their hair daily, change their clothes often, and take baths every Saturday. But evidence from Viking settlements in Orkney shows that they have lice and fleas all the same – just like everyone else in Scotland at this time.

And even if they are well groomed, they are not soft. Some kings, like Harold Fairhair, who rules Norway from AD 880 to 930, are said to use brutal methods to show who is in charge. According to sagas (histories in verse) composed by Viking settlers in Iceland, Harold cuts off the arms and legs of anyone who opposes him.

Why did the Vikings leave their homelands in Scandinavia?

- **Were they pirates?**
  Yes! 'Viking' means 'men from the bays' or 'coastal raiders'.

- **Did they want freedom?**
  Yes! From around AD 900, Viking kings in Norway and Iceland were trying to control warlords and their private armies, so many Vikings set sail for a new, free land.

- **Did they want land?**
  Yes! Compared with Norway, where most Vikings in Scotland came from, Scotland has a milder climate and good farmland.

- **Did they want wives?**
  Yes, yes, yes – and not just for Scotland! The Viking habit of killing unwanted girl babies at birth was leading to a shortage of women in Scandinavia. Vikings also raided Scotland for women to take to Iceland. DNA studies show that around one quarter of today's Scottish men have Viking ancestors, and that most of today's Icelanders are descended from Viking men and their Scottish wives.

AD 867–870

Vikings conquer the Anglian kingdom of Northumbria, and destroy Dumbarton, capital of the British kingdom of Strathclyde. They also take complete control of the Orkney and Shetland islands.

After fighting fiercely to win territory in the north and west of the Scottish mainland, Viking settlers seem to live fairly peacefully alongside their neighbours, the Picts and the Scots. The evidence of place names shows that villages inhabited by Picts and Scots continue to thrive alongside Viking ones.

But in Orkney and Shetland, Viking settlers take over completely. Most place names are now Viking, and new Viking buildings are constructed on top of older Pictish sites. Vikings import clothes, jewels, weapons and building materials – all from Norway. They also bring farm animals, including the ancestors of today's Shetland ponies, which were much bigger in Viking times. We know this because the Vikings used to eat them, and their bones have been found on Viking rubbish heaps.

What happens to the Picts who lived in Orkney and Shetland before the Vikings? Are they killed? Driven out? Made to work for Viking settlers? Or are they rounded up, shipped away to Scandinavia and sold as slaves? No-one knows. But one thing is for sure: they disappear – for ever.

Under one roof

Viking settlers bring their own building designs for homes with them – and their own house-mice. The mice stow away on ships; traces of their DNA can still be found in some Scottish mice today! Wherever Vikings settle in Scotland, they build long-houses. As the name suggests, these are long, narrow, single-storey buildings, made of stone, wood or turf. They have family living space at one end and byres (see page 119) for cattle and horses at the other.

Viking-style longhouses – also known as 'black houses' – are built in north and west Scotland until around 1900, and many are still standing today.

A dead cow above the door of a Viking longhouse was thought to bring good luck.

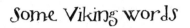

Some Viking words

'Byre' is the Viking word for 'stable'; it is still used to mean a cowshed in Scotland today. Other words brought to Scotland by the Vikings include:

- dale (valley)

- holm (island)

- ness (island)

- voe (sheltered harbour)

- wick (bay).

AD 892
Sigurd the Strong is killed – by his dead enemy!

Viking Earl Sigurd of Orkney is a mighty warrior. He conquers most of north Scotland and kills Maelbrige, leader of the Dál Riata army. Proudly, he cuts off Maelbrige's head and ties it to his saddle, as a splendid but grisly war trophy. As Sigurd gallops home, the head bounces up and down, and the teeth in its gaping mouth scratch him. To a brave Viking warrior like Sigurd, the wound seems like nothing – but it proves to be fatal. Germs from Maelbrige's mouth spread through Sigurd's blood, and poison him!

Bite, fright. Maelbrige gets his revenge.

AD 1004

The first Scots reach America. Their names are Haki and Hekja. They are slaves from Viking-ruled Scotland, and part of an expedition led by Icelander Thorfinn Karlsefni. He is hoping to find new places for Vikings to live, in Vinland (the Viking name for Newfoundland, Canada), but is driven away by bad weather, fights with Native Americans and quarrels among the settlers.

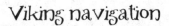

Viking navigation

How did the Vikings steer their ships across trackless seas and oceans?

- At night, by the stars; during the daytime, by the sun.
- By observing clouds which gather over hills.
- By bird-watching; some birds fly far out to sea, others stay close to land.
- By looking for seaweed, which grows in shallower seas around coasts.
- By sniffing for the smell of wet sheep, sheep-droppings, and the woodsmoke from houses, all carried on the breeze.
- By using rock crystal as a magnifying lens, rather like a telescope.

AD 1100

Svein Asleifarson, a satisfied Viking settler in Orkney, describes the perfect Viking year:

- **Winter:** at home, feasting with warriors
- **Early spring:** sowing crops on the farm
- **Late spring:** going on Viking raids to Ireland and the Hebrides
- **Summer:** at home, harvesting
- **Autumn:** raiding again!

CHAPTER NINE

FROM ALBA TO SCOTLAND

AD 842-1263

Meanwhile, the Picts, Scots, Britons and Angles have been defending their lands from the Vikings. They have also been fighting each other. It takes hundreds of years – until the 13th century – before Scotland becomes a united kingdom – and before it's called Scotland!

AD 842-847

Cinead Mac Ailpin (Kenneth MacAlpin) becomes King of the Picts – although he is from Dál Riata. Kenneth's mother is a Pictish princess, and so he claims the right to rule Pictish lands. After five years of fighting the

Picts, he invites the last surviving Pictish prince to peace talks – and kills him!

Picts in a pit? Possibly!

Some stories say that Kenneth invited the last Pictish prince and his warriors to a grand feast, and had a hidden pit dug under their side of the table. It was covered by a trap door. At the end of the meal, Kenneth's servants opened the trap door and the Picts fell into the pit, where they were trapped and killed.

AD 850
Kenneth controls all Scotland north of the River Clyde – except where the Vikings are starting to settle. But not for long….

Dál Riata is threatened by a massive Viking fleet of 140 ships. It's time to move some more holy bones! For safety, Kenneth brings the body of St Columba from Iona to Pictland. It is buried at Dunkeld.

The Vikings come to raid and conquer. But their attacks are producing another, unexpected, result. Instead of fighting each other, the two largest, most powerful Scottish peoples, the Picts and the Scots, are having to unite to survive.

AD 858

Where has Pictland gone? The Pictish language and culture are disappearing…

As a Scot, Kenneth MacAlpin speaks Gaelic (the Celtic language used in Dál Riata), and follows Dál Riata customs and traditions. So do his warriors, and anyone else who wants to win favour with him. By the time he dies, in 858, Gaelic is spreading through Pictland, along with many Dál Riata laws.

AD 859–900

Being royal is a dangerous business. None of the next six kings lives for long:

- 859–863 Donald I: murdered
- 863–877 Constantine I: killed by Vikings
- 877–878 Aed: murdered by cousin and rival, Giric
- 878–889 Eochan & Giric: probably murdered
- 889–900 Donald II: poisoned

AD 900–943

New king Constantine II gives his kingdom a new name: Alba (a Gaelic word that probably means 'Mountain Land'). The new name is to show that it is a single nation – a nation with grand ambitions!

Constantine II – and the kings who rule after him – face many challenges:

- Keep out Viking invaders!
- Unite Pictland and Dál Riata!
- Conquer land from the Angles!
- Battle against the Britons!
- Fight rebellious mormaers (nobles) in the north-east!
- Reorganise the Church!
- Produce an heir!
- Stay alive!

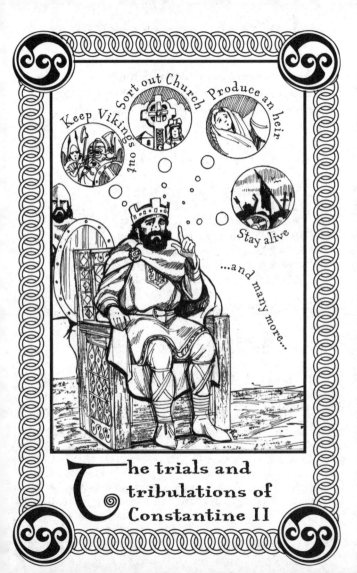

Keep Vikings out

Sort out Church

Produce an heir

Stay alive

...and many more...

The trials and tribulations of Constantine II

AD 943

Constantine II has survived for 43 years – a
record among Scottish kings so far! He retires
and spends the rest of his life as a monk.

AD 943–1005

The next seven kings all die horribly:

- 943–954 Malcolm I: killed in battle
- 954–962 Indulf: killed in battle
- 962–967 Dubh: killed in a fight
- 967–971 Culen: killed in a fight
- 971–995 Kenneth II: murdered
- 995–997 Constantine III: murdered
- 997–1005 Kenneth III: murdered

Shot by his own statue!

It happened like this – or so old stories say.
Kenneth II killed the son of Fenella, the
daughter of the Earl of Angus. To get revenge,
Fenella first had a very lifelike statue of
Kenneth made, which showed him holding a
gleaming golden apple. Next, Fenella invited
Kenneth to a great feast at her castle. After the
meal, she invited him to take the precious apple,
as a gift. Alas, it was a trick! The statue was
booby-trapped. As soon as Kenneth touched the
apple, he was shot and killed by hidden arrows.

AD 1010
The new king, Malcolm II 'The Destroyer', defeats a Viking army at Mortlach, Banffshire. After the battle, Malcolm pays for a church, called Mortlach, to give thanks for his victory. The skulls of dead Viking warriors are used to help build the walls.

AD 1018
King Malcolm and King Owen 'the Bald' of Strathclyde capture Northumbria. Alba is getting bigger!

AD 1030
But soon it's smaller again! Thorfinn the Mighty, Earl of Orkney, wins control of all northern Scotland.

As well as fighting Alba, Vikings living in Scotland also attack Vikings from Ireland and the Isle of Man. They even go on raids to plunder peaceful Viking villages in Norway.

AD 1034
Malcolm II dies at Glamis Castle – perhaps in a hunting accident, or perhaps he is murdered. His blood is still said to bubble up through the floor of the castle's great hall.

AD 1034

King Owen the Bald dies and his kingdom of Strathclyde passes to Duncan, Malcolm II's grandson and heir (Duncan's father is dead). Duncan's kingdom of Alba stretches as far south as the River Tweed – the modern border with England. But most people in Scotland still call their homeland 'Alba', because they speak Gaelic. 'Scotland' is an Anglo-Saxon word, used by the English.

AD 1040

Duncan is killed in battle by Macbeth, mormaer (nobleman) of Moray. Macbeth is older, more experienced, and a better warrior than Duncan, and now becomes king himself.

The Borders: A bad place to be!

For the next 500 years and more, English and Scottish armies fought over Border territory – the lands between the River Tyne and the River Forth. Soldiers from both sides advanced, attacked and retreated, as neither side could win a lasting victory. They destroyed houses, set fire to farms, drove away livestock and killed innocent civilians. One of the worst war crimes took place at Berwick on Tweed in 1296, when 16,000 peaceful men, women and children were massacred by the English.

The real Macbeth?

Around 1605, over 500 years after Macbeth died, English dramatist William Shakespeare wrote a play about him. Shakespeare knew very little about the real Macbeth, and portrayed him as a weak, wicked man, a murderer, and a friend of witches. He got the geography of Scotland wrong, as well.

In fact, Macbeth was one of the best kings that Alba had. His fame survived for centuries. Chroniclers in Scotland – writing shortly before Shakespeare – described him as 'red, tall, golden-haired and furious (i.e. brave in battle)'.

Macbeth DID NOT:
- Murder King Duncan in his bed
- Have a wicked, scheming wife
- Go half-mad with guilt
- See moving forests and ghostly daggers.

Macbeth DID:
- Rule well and bring peace, for a while
- Give land and money to the Church (as did his wife)
- Go on a pilgrimage to the holy city of Rome. There, priests said he scattered money 'like seeds' to all the poor beggars.
- Defend Alba from English kings
- Make friends with the Vikings in Orkney.

Which witch?

In Shakespeare's play, Macbeth meets three witches: they are scary and spooky. However, in Macbeth's time, it was believed that witches could help as well as harm. They made medicines and love potions, cured sick cattle, raised winds, and had magic Serpent Stones to treat dangerous injuries.

Special 'clootie wells' (cloth wells) also featured in good witches' healing rituals. Sufferers from disease dipped clothes in the well water, then hung them up nearby. As the cloth decayed, they hoped their disease would also fade away.

AD 1057

Duncan's son Malcolm kills Macbeth at the battle of Lumphanan. After the battle, the soldiers bring Macbeth's head to Malcolm on a plate. The next heir – Macbeth's stepson – is conveniently murdered, and Malcolm (nicknamed Canmore – 'Big Head' or 'Great Chief') becomes King Malcom III.

The real Macbeth ruled Scotland more or less peacefully for 17 years and gave generously to the Church and the poor.

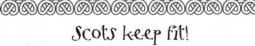

Scots keep fit!

The very first Highland Games may have been held while Malcolm's army was waiting to fight Macbeth. According to legend, Malcolm organised races and other competitions to test the strength and fitness of his soldiers.

Malcolm's men must have been very tough. Their camp was at Braemar, the coldest place in Britain. The lowest ever British temperature was recorded there in 1982: minus 17°C.

Highland Games were banned after the Jacobite Rebellion of 1745 (see Volume 2), but the Braemar games were started again in 1832 and still continue today.

AD 1066
Vikings from Norway invade Yorkshire, and are defeated by soldiers from Scotland and England, fighting side by side.

fairy magic

At Dunvegan Castle, on the Isle of Skye, there is a tattered, faded banner: the Fairy Flag of the MacLeods. It is made of silk from the Middle East, woven around AD 700. It was probably captured from defeated Vikings in 1066, but old legends tell a stranger story...

They say the Flag once belonged to a fairy-woman, married to the MacLeod chief. After 20 years, she left him and returned to Fairyland – but the Flag remained, and has magic powers to save the Scottish people from danger. It can be used three times only and has already brought victory twice, in 1490 and 1580. Will it ever be used again?

AD 1066–1068

Normans (people of Viking origin settled in France) conquer England. English Prince Edgar, his mother, and his sister Margaret escape and head for Scotland. The women are shipwrecked near Dunfermline.

Margaret is young, beautiful, clever, and King Malcolm falls in love with her. They marry and have eight children. For centuries after,

Queen Margaret's nightdress is borrowed by Scottish queens to protect them from the dangers of childbirth. Margaret gives most of her children English names, to annoy the French-speaking Normans.

Margaret turns Dunfermline Castle from a scruffy soldiers' mess into a richly decorated palace. She bans all dirty, smelly, badly dressed people; she wants respect and good manners.

Margaret also brings priests and monks – who can read and write, unlike king Malcolm! – to say prayers, teach the royal children, and help run the government.

Good Queen Margaret

It is said that Margaret:

- Read holy books with jewelled covers.
- Fed 20 beggars' babies every day, with a golden spoon.
- Made Sunday a public holiday for everyone.
- Paid for a ferry to help pilgrims reach St Andrew's tomb.
- Spent hours in a damp, dark cave, praying.

Unsurprisingly, she was made a saint in 1250.

AD 1072

The Normans invade Scotland. They force Malcolm to accept King William the Conqueror of England as his overlord. This is very dangerous for the Scots. It means that future kings of England will claim to rule the kingdom of Alba!

When Malcolm is killed fighting in 1093, Queen Margaret dies of a broken heart. As her coffin is carried past his tomb, it mysteriously becomes too heavy to move – and so they are buried side by side.

AD 1098

Meanwhile, in the north of Scotland, Viking earl Magnus Barelegs wants more land.

Edgar the Peaceable now rules the kingdom of Alba – and he does not like fighting. He tells Magnus that he may have all the Scottish land he can sail around. Magnus sails round all the Hebrides islands, then gets his men to carry his boat across a narrow strip of land in the far south-west – and wins the Mull of Kintyre (the tip of the Kintyre peninsula) as well!

Magnus Barelegs wore a sort of kilt, not typical Viking trousers. This is one of the first-known references to kilts in Scotland.

The voyage of Magnus Barelegs

Outer Hebrides

Inner Hebrides

Mull of Kintyre

AD 1093–1124

Malcolm III dies – and leaves six squabbling sons, plus his own ambitious brother and nephew. All want to be king. There is war, and there are horrible murders, as they all fight for the throne. The kingdom of Alba is divided.

AD 1124–1153

A surprise! The hated Normans arrive in Scotland – but as guests, not enemies!

How and why? David I, Malcolm III's last surviving son, has spent years in England hiding from his brothers. Now that he's king, David invites English and Norman knights to help him control his kingdom. He gives them estates in southern Scotland, and they build fine castles and churches. So does David himself, who founds seven monasteries. Poor farmers in Scotland have to live and work on castle and monastery land – most unwillingly.

Multilingual Scotland

By this point five languages are spoken in Scotland: Gaelic (in the north), Norse (by the Vikings), Latin (by priests and monks), English (in the south) and Norman French (by the Normans). A sixth language, Scots, is beginning to develop as all these mix together. Though closely related to English, it also contains a few words from Pictish and British, which have almost disappeared by now. Traders soon bring a seventh language, Dutch (also related to English), from across the North Sea.

As the Scots language becomes more popular, so does a new name for the kingdom of Alba. It is 'Scotland' – an English word based on the old Roman name (Scoti) for the people of Dál Riata.

AD 1136
The oldest-known Scottish business is recorded. It's the Aberdeen Harbour Board, still going strong today.

Around this time, the first towns are built in Scotland. King David is keen to encourage trade. Scots merchants sell fish, hides, wool – and coal, from Scotland's first mines. Most of their customers are from the Netherlands.

Dutch merchants and sailors come to live in Scotland's east-coast ports.

David also gives orders for minting the first Scottish coins. Before his reign, Scottish traders had to use Roman, English or Scandinavian money.

AD 1174–1214
Trade brings wealth, and David's new clerks – and Norman knights – have brought law and order. But then the next king, William 'the Lyon', loses Scotland's independence – by invading England, getting captured, and being forced to swear loyalty to the English king.

By good luck, William the Lyon is able to buy Scotland's freedom back, by paying a huge ransom to English king Richard I (known as 'the Lionheart'). Richard wants the money to go on Crusade.

Lions were clearly high fashion in royal circles; both kings had fierce roaring lions as their heraldic badges. The Lion Rampant is still the standard (personal flag) of the Scottish monarch today.

The Scottish standard is described in the language of heraldry as:

Or, a lion rampant Gules armed and langued Azure within a double tressure flory counter-flory Gules

or, in plain English:

Yellow, with a rearing lion in red, with blue claws and tongue, within a red double border with fleurs-de-lys facing in opposite directions.

AD 1214–1286

Like father, like son. The next two kings, Alexander II and III, build fearsome royal castles, quell rebellions, and keep English invaders out of Scotland by making love (that is, arranging marriage alliances) as well as war. They are also great lawmakers who protect the Church and encourage learning.

AD 1263

Thanks to bad weather, which wrecks Viking ships as they attack, Alexander III wins a great sea-battle at Largs, in south-west Scotland. The Vikings retreat, and Viking kings give up most of their Scottish lands. The kingdom of Alba now includes the Hebrides and the Isle of Man. Only Orkney and Shetland in the far north are still ruled by Vikings.

Viking leader King Haakon IV dies. He is buried twice: once in Orkney, while his ships wait all winter, trapped by storms; and once back in his proper home of Norway.

Now Alba (almost) equals Scotland!

Strange Scottish scholars

John Duns Scotus (c.1266–1308) was one of the most brilliant men of his age. A Franciscan friar, he studied philosophy, psychology, ethics, linguistics and religion.

BUT he was so clever that – as a joke – his name was given to very stupid people, or 'dunces'.

Michael Scot (1175–c.1232) – another churchman – was also a wonderful scholar. He was tutor to the Holy Roman Emperor, and translated world-famous scientific books from Arabic into Latin. He travelled to Spain, and learned Hebrew, mathematics and medicine.

BUT he was so clever that people said he must be a wizard. They claimed he tamed demons, split the Eildon Hills (in southern Scotland) into three, and could foretell the future. He even predicted how he would be killed – by a stone falling on his head. He made a metal helmet for protection – but still a stone killed him! By chance, one hurtled from a church roof as he walked underneath.

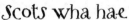

Scots wha hae

One of the most famous Scottish poems, about one of Scotland's most famous battles, by Scotland's most famous poet. Robert the Bruce rouses his men before the Battle of Bannockburn:

Scots, wha hae wi' Wallace bled,
Scots, wham Bruce has aften led,
Welcome to your gory bed
Or to victorie.

Now's the day and now's the hour;
See the front of battle lour;
See approach proud Edward's power –
Chains and slaverie!

Wha will be a traitor knave?
Wha can fill a coward's grave?
Wha sae base as be a slave?
Let him turn and flee!

…

Lay the proud usurpers low!
Tyrants fall in every foe!
Liberty's in every blow!
Let us do, or die!

Robert Burns, 1759–1796

[wha = who; hae = have; wi' = with; wham = whom; aften = often; gory bed = bloody death; front = face; lour = scowl; proud Edward = Edward I of England; wha = who; knave = criminal; wha sae base = who's so low]

CHAPTER TEN

WARS OF INDEPENDENCE

AD 1286-1392

Scotland is finally named Scotland – and includes all of modern Scotland except Orkney and Shetland. But this does not mean that Scottish kings are always in control of all their kingdom, because threats to their power come from two directions at once.

In the west and the north, mighty nobles have ambitions to rule little kingdoms of their own. Far south, across the border, English kings, especially warlike Edward I (who came to power in 1272), have plans to conquer all of Scotland. Edward's nickname? The 'Hammer of the Scots'!

AD 1286

It's a wild, rainy night and King Alexander III is in a royal hurry.

He sets off from Edinburgh to his castle at Dunfermline, where his young and charming new wife is waiting for him. What happens next is uncertain, but some stories say that a haggard old crone sidles up to the King and whispers an awful warning: 'Cross the water tonight,' she croaks, 'and you'll never return...' Ignoring her prophecy, Alexander takes the ferry and rides on homewards.

But he loses his way in the dark, and he and his horse are found at the bottom of a cliff the next morning – very, very dead.

Alexander's death causes a royal crisis for Scotland. By the laws of inheritance, the next new ruler should be Alexander's closest living relative – his second cousin. But there are three problems with this plan. Alexander's cousin is a girl (called Margaret); she lives far away (in Norway, where her father is king); and she's only three years old!

Alexander III never made it home.

Back home in Scotland there are 13 rival nobles, all wanting to be king. And to make matters more difficult, England's King Edward I has decided that his son must marry Margaret, 'the Maid of Norway'. That way, he thinks, England can take control of Scotland without any fighting.

AD 1290
The Maid of Norway, now aged six, boards a boat headed for Scotland.

She has a plate of royal sweeties to comfort her – but the ship hits a storm! The winds and waves are treacherous and terrifying. Poor little Margaret dies – of severe seasickness, they say – as her ship reaches Orkney.

AD 1292
Someone has to rule Scotland – so who should be king?

One Scottish noble, John Balliol, has the backing of King Edward I of England – the most powerful man in four kingdoms, with a whole army at his command – and soon becomes king. Balliol is descended from a noble Norman family, who came to Scotland when David I was king. Rival Scots nobles are not happy, but are not strong enough to fight against Edward.

In return for Edward's help, Balliol swears loyalty to him as overlord. This means an end to Scotland's independence…

…but then Edward pushes Balliol too far by insisting that the Scots help him fight their long-term friend and ally, France. (Of course, the French are Balliol's kin.)

AD 1295
Balliol refuses. Defiantly, he signs a treaty of friendship with France. The Auld Alliance is born (see next page).

AD 1296
Edward I of England invades Scotland. Balliol surrenders – and, as a sign of shame, he is stripped of his crown, sceptre, sword, ring and rich royal robes, complete with their Scottish kingly badge – the rampant lion. From now on, Balliol is known to Scots as 'toom tabard' (empty coat).

The Auld Alliance

Now remembered as the start of the 'Auld Alliance', Balliol's treaty is the first of many agreements between Scotland and France. In these bargains of friendship, both sides promise help to each other – especially against England. Edward – and later English kings – are furious. France is the richest, strongest nation in medieval Europe, and home to an advanced, sophisticated culture. It is also England's sworn enemy. The Auld Alliance traps England between two troublesome, hostile nations, and means that it has two long borders, hundreds of miles apart, to defend.

The Auld Alliance gives Scotland many advantages: as well as gaining protection from a bigger, stronger neighbour, Scots people also establish close links with the French – first through trade and warfare, later through scholarship, art, architecture and royal marriages (which promise much but often prove problematic).

From 1296, Scottish merchants and nobles import enormous quantities of French wine, legally – and sponsoring French pirates who attack English trading ships. In 1539, for example, Scots Cardinal Beaton purchases an astounding 165,000 bottles of claret (red wine) for his household. Colonies of Scots also move to live in wine-growing regions of south-west France (there is a whole Scottish suburb of Bordeaux), buying vineyards, making wine, speaking French and paying French taxes.

Thousands of Scottish mercenary soldiers emigrate to fight in France, often against the English. The Garde Écossaise (Scots Guard) is founded in 1415 and remains a part of the French Army until after the French Revolution of 1789. Small numbers of expert French warriors visit Scotland to advise Scottish army commanders in the 1290s. But they find the Scots savage and backward, and are pleased when it's time to head home.

After Balliol's surrender. Edward takes control of the southern half of Scotland and captures the sacred Stone of Destiny. That's what he claims, anyway...

Did Scottish monks hide the real Stone of Destiny?

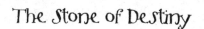

The Stone of Destiny

From AD 843 to 1292, all kings in Scotland were crowned while seated on this stone. It was brought to Scone, in central Scotland, by Kenneth MacAlpin, the first king to rule both Dál Riata and Pictland (see pages 123–124).

After capturing it in 1296, Edward I's troops announced that they were taking it away to London, where it became part of the coronation throne used by all English kings and queens. But Scottish legends tell how the real stone was hidden by the monks of Scone Abbey, who gave the English a fake stone instead – some say, an old stone drain-cover from the monks' lavatory! The Scottish legends say that they hid the original on Dunsinnan Hill – or possibly under Rosslyn Chapel, near Edinburgh.

The Stone of Destiny (real or fake) was 'kidnapped' from Westminster Abbey in London by Scottish students in 1950. It was found in Arbroath Abbey, returned to London, and then officially given back to Scotland in 1996. Today, it is on display in Edinburgh Castle. Scientific tests have suggested that it may be the real Stone of Destiny after all.

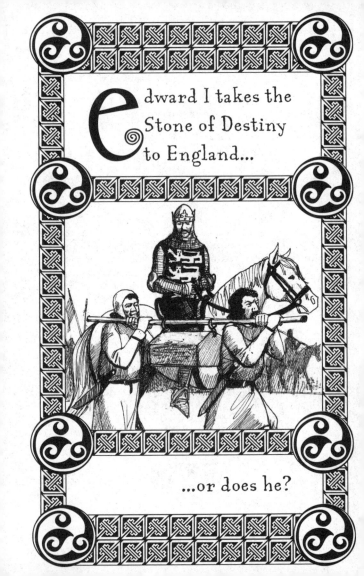

edward I takes the Stone of Destiny to England...

...or does he?

from outlaw to hero

AD 1297

The second son of a Lowland knight gets into a fight with some Englishmen in Lanark. His name is William Wallace, and he is helped to escape by a woman (possibly his wife). She is killed by the sheriff's men, who are meant to keep law and order. In return, Wallace kills the sheriff. Wallace is outlawed, with a price on his head. With nothing to lose – and a hatred of English royal officers like the sheriff – he joins the fight against England.

For months, Wallace lives on the run, planning attacks on the English together with a fierce Highland warlord, Sir Andrew Murray. Their chance comes in September 1297. The mighty English army camps near Stirling – still to this day the strategic 'Gateway to the Highlands' – where Edward I is trying to smash his way into the castle with the 'War Wolf', his most monstrous siege engine. Wallace and Murray are outnumbered, but are determined to fight. When the English send ambassadors (monks on donkeys – symbols of weakness) inviting the Scots to surrender, Wallace replies: 'We are not here to talk peace but to do battle and liberate our country!'

Stirring words, but how can he possibly win? Three things turn the odds in his favour:

- Wallace hides his army in a wood. Advantage Scotland!
- The English commander, the earl of Surrey, oversleeps. Bad move, England!
- The English hurry across Stirling Bridge. Bold but foolish!

Wallace makes his men wait until half the English are across – then they charge! The English are trapped. They can't go backwards or forwards. Either way they die – speared by the Scots as they try to retreat across the bridge, or crushed by their panicking comrades. The rest of the English army is still on the far side of the river, and has to watch, powerless to help them. It's a Scottish victory!

One English leader, Hugh de Cressingham, is killed – and his fate after death is gruesome. Wallace's men strip the skin from his body and share it out as souvenirs! Wallace himself

Battle of Stirling
Bridge, 1297

has a sword-belt made from the skin, and wears it as a proud trophy. Understandably but unheroically, the earl of Surrey rides away so fast that his horse drops dead under him.

From this horror, it is easy to see how the Scots got their wild, bloodthirsty reputation. But English soldiers could be savage, too; in fact, the Scots claimed that English soldiers had tails – they were animals, not humans.

AD 1298

Wallace's triumph is short-lived. His Scottish 'schiltrons' (hedgehog-like clusters of spearmen) are shot to pieces at Falkirk by English bowmen. This is the first time the English have used their terrible new longbows in Scotland, and they are delighted by the carnage they cause.

AD 1305

After years of hit-and-run raids on the English, Wallace is finally betrayed and captured. He is carted off to London, and executed most horribly. First he is dragged through the streets behind a horse – in a thick leather wrapping, so that he suffers but survives. Then he is hanged, drawn and quartered. The separate sections of his body are sent to Scotland, and put on display as a ghastly warning.

G'day, mate!

Books, songs, poems and blockbuster films praise Wallace as one of Scotland's greatest heroes. It is strange but perhaps inevitable that a statue below the massive Wallace monument at Stirling is modelled on Australian movie star Mel Gibson.

A group of Scots, averse to this cinematisation of history, protested at the likeness. Soon the statue had to be cordoned off to protect it from vandalism. Strange that a statue proclaiming 'FREEDOM' should have to be locked behind bars for its own protection!

Time for a new hero!

AD 1305

Scotland has a new king: Robert the Bruce. Like Wallace, Robert is of Norman descent and from the Lowlands. Also like Wallace, Bruce is tough and ruthless – but he's less of a patriot than Wallace. With lands in the Borders, he shifts alliegance several times before deciding to be Scottish.

AD 1306

Bruce is the great-great-grandson of King David I. But other men have better claims to the throne. He meets one rival, Red John Comyn, in church in Dumfries – which should be a holy place of safety. Bruce stabs Red John Comyn to death – then gets himself crowned King Robert I as soon as possible.

Bruce loses his next battles against the English – some say this is God's punishment for murder. He flees to a cave to hide. Where? Perhaps Rathlin Island in Ulster, or somewhere in the Orkneys, or even Ardnamurchan. No-one knows for certain.

What women want...

Possibly, Bruce inherited his ruthless streak from his mother, the Countess of Carrick. Before Bruce was born, she is said to have seen a handsome knight, much younger than she was, riding past her castle – and kidnapped him. He became Bruce's father.

Saved by a spider?

Robert the Bruce features in one of Scotland's most famous stories. While hiding in his cave, tired and despondent, he saw a spider spinning a web. Six times it tried and failed to span a crevice, but at last it succeeded. 'Try, try and try again!' thought Bruce, realising he couldn't give up so easily.

'Try, try, and try again!' is an inspiring motto for a small, weak, 14th-century kingdom threatened by a stronger neighbour. It is a shame, then, that it was probably invented over 500 years later – by the great Scottish novelist Sir Walter Scott (see Volume 2).

Try, try, and try again!

AD 1306

While Bruce is in hiding, King Edward I of England takes vengeance. Three of Bruce's brothers are executed – and his sister, Mary, is hung for months in a cage from the walls of Roxburgh Castle. Amazingly, she survives.

Although terribly cold, wet and windy, a cage is probably healthier than Scotland's castle prisons! The fearsome Bottle Dungeon at St Andrews, for example, is shaped like a flask, with no light, no windows, and only one narrow opening. Scotland's friends, the French, have a grim name for this sort of prison – *oubliette*. It means 'a place to be forgotten in'.

AD 1307

Edward I of England dies. He has vowed not to be buried until he has defeated the Scots, so his body remains above ground, in a raised tomb.

AD 1314

Edward's son, Edward II, is no warrior. The Scots raid far south across the border – and Bruce wins a glorious victory at Bannockburn near Stirling.

Like Wallace, Bruce chooses the site of his battle very carefully: boggy ground beside a burn (stream). He sets traps for the English, digging pits and scattering caltrops (cruel metal spikes that maim horses). English knights, who ride huge steeds and wear heavy chain mail, cannot charge to attack here. Instead, they stumble and fall, trampling each other to death.

Bruce also inspires his troops by a brilliant start to the battle. When the English champion, with his big horse and splendid armour, gallops out to challenge him, Bruce leaps from his nimble Scottish pony, swings his battle-axe, and splits the the champion's head in two!

Declaration of Arbroath

AD 1320

Battles aren't enough to keep a kingdom safe. Scotland needs the Church – and international Church law – to back it. Thirty-nine top Scots nobles write to the Pope in Rome, asking him to stop supporting England's invasions, and recognise Scotland as a free, independent nation. Their words, preserved in a document called the Declaration of Arbroath, echo down the centuries:

'So long as a hundred of us remain alive, we fight, not for glory nor for riches nor for honour, but only and alone for freedom, which no good man surrenders but with his life.'

Scotland after Bruce

AD 1328
At last, the new English king, Edward III, makes a truce with Scotland...

AD 1329
...but the next year, King Robert the Bruce dies – not in battle, but of leprosy.

Leprosy is a cruel killer, but Bruce is luckier than most lepers. They're banned from Scottish towns, and have to carry clappers made of wood to warn people that they are approaching. They shelter in hovels outside town walls and survive by begging – or by eating food that's too bad to be put on sale in town markets.

The name 'leprosy' covers a range of skin diseases in Bruce's time, some mild and some very serious. Traditional treatments include medicines made from plants, gold, spiders, and water from holy – or magic – wells. The Liberton Well in Edinburgh is famous for treating skin ailments. Its waters are naturally oily and may really have soothing properties.

Heart to heart

Bruce said that he wanted his dead body to go on a crusade. This proved impossible, but his heart was taken to Spain, where Christians were fighting Muslims. But the soldier carrying Bruce's heart was killed and it was returned to Scotland. It was sealed in a lead casket and buried at Melrose Abbey – where it has recently been rediscovered.

Bruce's heart was not the only Scottish body part to be treated so strangely. Grieving widow Devorgilla Balliol wore her dead husband's heart like a jewel – and founded Sweetheart Abbey near Dumfries as a place where it, and she, could be buried.

AD 1329–1371

David, son of Robert the Bruce, becomes king. He's five years old – and already married! (To Joanna, seven-year-old sister of king Edward III, as part of a peace agreement.)

As a powerless child, David II faces many threats, especially from the ambitious Balliol family (see pages 150–151). They seize power, and David, aged 10, is sent to France for safety. He returns in 1341 together with the French, who are again at war with England.

This time, the Auld Alliance is not much help to Scotland. As David leads Scots and French troops against England, he is captured by the English and spends the next 11 years in prison. While he's locked up, a new force – his nephew, Robert Stewart – takes control of Scotland (see Volume 2).

AD 1338

The English invade again. They besiege important Scottish castles, including Dunbar. They expect that it will be easy to capture – because a woman, Countess 'Black Agnes'

Randolph, has been left in charge. They are wrong! Agnes turns out to be a master of practical – and psychological – warfare. She sends her men to drop huge rocks to crush English siege engines – and her maids to sweep the castle battlements, as if the war were nothing but a dusty nuisance. Agnes defends the castle for 10 long months, until Scottish help arrives. Her soldiers taunt the retreating English with this song:

> 'Came I early, came I late,
> I found Agnes at the gate!'

AD 1349–50, 1361–2, 1379, 1392...

A devastating new enemy attacks Scotland – but it doesn't carry a sword. It's plague! The Black Death!

At first, Scots soldiers fighting south of the border jeer when they see their English enemies dropping like flies from this fatal new illness. But they soon catch the plague from English fleas, and take it home to Scotland. There, it spreads very quickly. Scotland's cold climate means that the fiercest, most contagious 'pneumonic' form of the disease

Puir wee
fleabitten
Sassenachs!

develops. It is passed on by coughs and sneezes, and victims are reported to 'swell up and die' within two days. As plague returns again and again, around one third of the Scottish population perishes. There is widespread suffering and starvation, as food crops go unharvested – and there are rumours of cannibalism among survivors.

The state of the nation

The plague was a nightmare, but, even before it arrived, everyday life for medieval Scottish people was 'short, sharp and brutal'. Archaeological evidence – from skeletons to fossilised middens (rubbish pits) – tells us that Scots of that era were smaller than today – about 5 ft 6 in (168 cm) for men, and 5 ft 2 in (158 cm) for women – and much more likely to die young. Up to half of all children born failed to reach 15, with most dying, before they were 5 years old, from coughs, colds and stomach infections. Men and women were considered old if they reached 45, and decrepit by 67, but many did not survive that long.

Around one third of all women died in pregnancy or childbirth; men often died fighting, or from accidents on farms. Dangerous infections, such as smallpox and TB, killed many others. All kinds of parasites, including lice, fleas and intestinal worms, made medieval lives uncomfortable. And poor hygiene was always a problem. Town streets streamed with sewage and were heaped with decaying rubbish. There were springs and wells, but no running water. Lavatories were stinking pits with only moss for toilet paper.

Hunger and poor nourishment could also be deadly. There was good food in Scotland, but not everyone got enough. Poor people lived mostly on cereals – porridge or flat, dry cakes made of oats or barley. If they were lucky, they added butter or cheese, a few garden vegetables – mainly leeks, cabbage, kale and 'cybo' (spring onions) – and wild foods such as berries, nuts and fungi. Only the rich could afford expensive, exotic imports, such as spices, apples or onions. Meat was a treat. Rich Scots ate beef, pork, mutton, goat and venison – and the poor hoped to!

Blood Puddings (like sausages)
These were made whenever a farm animal was killed. Medieval people could not afford to waste anything edible.

1 Put the blood in a bowl. Stir well.
2 Add salt, milk, chopped fat, chopped onions, oatmeal, herbs or spices.
3 Pack into cleaned animal intestines.
4 Put into boiling water and boil for half an hour.
5 Store in a cool, airy place, and boil again before eating.

Cream Crowdie
This is still enjoyed today, ideally with fresh Scottish raspberries.

1 Toast some oatmeal on an iron girdle (griddle) and let it cool.
2 Whip some cream into a froth.
3 Arrange thick layers of cream and thin layers of oatmeal alternately in a bowl.
4 Drizzle fragrant heather honey on top.

Black Bun
Traditionally eaten at Hogmanay (New Year). It uses expensive luxury ingredients imported from southern Europe and faraway Asia.

1 Put raisins, currants, candied orange peel, almonds, spices (cloves, ginger, cinnamon, pepper) and flour in a big bowl.
2 Add buttermilk or beaten eggs and stir.
3 Line a baking tin with pastry. Put the fruit mixture inside.

4 Add a 'lid' of pastry, and seal the edges well.
5 Bake in a gentle oven for 4 hours.

Sowans (Soo-an)
Said to be good for invalids.

1 Soak oat grain husks in water for 3 days or
  more, until they smell sour.
2 Squeeze the husks to press out a milky liquid,
  then throw them away.
3 Stand the milky liquid in a jar in a warm
  place for 24 hours. You should find a thick
  layer at the bottom, and a thin liquid on top.
4 To eat, mix some of the thick layer with
  water then boil it, stirring, for 10 minutes.
  Serve with milk.

Roast Venison

For families with plenty of money, and lots of
kitchen servants.

1 Take a haunch (upper half of back leg) of a
  red deer.
2 Soak it for 6 hours in red wine mixed with
  vinegar.
3 Fix it on a spit (revolving metal pole) above a
  big, hot fire.
4 Mix the wine and vinegar with melted
  butter, and pour this over the haunch all the
  time as it turns.
5 When the haunch is nearly cooked, coat it
  with more butter, and sprinkle it with flour.
  Cook for another 15 minutes. This will give
  it a crispy coating.

Timeline of Scottish history

from ancient times to the coming of the Stewarts

c.12,000–11,000 BC First humans visit Scotland.

c.8500 BC Early hunters camp near present-day Edinburgh.

c.7000–5000 BC Humans begin to live in Scotland all year round.

c.6000 BC At the end of the Ice Age, rising sea levels eliminate the land bridge between the British Isles and continental Europe. A giant tsunami hits the east coast of Scotland.

c.5000–4000 BC New settlers arrive from north-west Spain.

c.4500–3000 BC First permanent villages; beginnings of farming and weaving; stone tools in use.

c.3800 BC Scotland's largest timber building constructed: Balbridie Hall, Aberdeenshire.

c.3100 BC Stone houses with built-in furniture built at Skara Brae, Orkney. Tomb of the Eagles built on South Ronaldsay, Orkney.

c.3000–2500 BC Stone monuments appear: barrows, cairns, chamber tombs, standing stones.

c.2700 BC Maes Howe tomb built on mainland Orkney.

c.2500 BC Stone circles built at Brodgar (Shetland) and Callanish.

c.2500–1000 BC Beginnings of metalworking in Scotland. High-quality bronze items appear at burial sites.

c.1600 BC Mummies buried at Cladh Hallan, South Uist, Outer Hebrides.

1159 BC Volcanic eruption in Iceland causes cooling of Scottish climate.

c.1100 BC Large numbers of children buried in a cave near Lossiemouth.

c.750 BC Celtic hillfort built at Eildon Hill near Melrose. Beginnings of ironworking in Scotland.

c.100 BC Broch built at Mousa, Shetland. Foundries and workshops built at Inverness. Foxes and badgers farmed for fur in Orkney.

AD 43 Romans successfully invade the British Isles.

AD 79 Romans survey the Scottish coast and begin to build camps and forts.

AD 84 Celts fight Romans at Mons Graupius; Romans claim a decisive victory.

AD 86–87 Romans abandon their fort at Inchtuthil near Perth.

AD 108 An entire Roman legion goes missing, allegedly slaughtered in Scotland.

AD 122–128 Romans build Hadrian's Wall.

AD 139–143 Romans build Antonine Wall.

AD 161–163 Romans abandon Antonine Wall.

AD 208–211 Roman emperor Septimius Severus tries to subdue northern Scotland and dies in the attempt.

AD 209 Earliest known mention of the Picts.

AD 342 First appearance of raiders from Ireland, called Scots.

c.AD 403 The future St Patrick is kidnapped and taken to Ireland.

AD 410 Romans abandon Hadrian's Wall.

c.AD 500 First Christian missionaries arrive in Scotland.

AD 563 St Columba builds his monastery on Iona.

AD 565 Earliest known mention of the Loch Ness Monster.

c.AD 600 First introduction of oats to Scotland.

AD 638 Angles conquer the British fort at Edinburgh; Britons make Stirling their capital.

AD 663 Synod of Whitby instructs the Scottish and Irish churches to adopt the practices of the Roman church.

AD 681 Picts launch a naval attack on Orkney.

AD 685 Pictish king Bridei defeats the Angles at the Battle of Dunnichen.

AD 697 Adhomnan of Iona writes 'The Law of the Innocent', a declaration of human rights.

AD 733 Relics of St Andrew arrive in Scotland.

AD 735 Pictish soldiers see a saltire (St Andrew's cross) in the sky. It becomes the national emblem of Scotland.

AD 740 The Picts conquer the Scots.

AD 795–826 Vikings repeatedly raid St Columba's monastery on Iona.

AD 839 Pictish leaders wiped out by Vikings.

AD 842 Cinead (Kenneth) MacAlpin crowned king of Picts and Scots at Scone.

AD 843 Picts and Scots unite to form the kingdom later known as Alba. From now until 1292, Scottish kings are crowned on the Stone of Destiny.

AD 847 Kenneth MacAlpin eliminates his Pictish rivals.

AD 850 Remains of St Columba moved from Iona to Dunkeld because of a threatened Viking invasion.

AD 867–870 Vikings capture Strathclyde, Orkney and Shetland.

AD 870 Vikings attack the convent at Coldingham, Berwickshire, where the nuns mutilate themselves to discourage their captors.

AD 892 Strange death of Viking earl Sigurd the Strong.

AD 900 New king Constantine II names his kingdom Alba.

c.AD 950 St Andrew's day becomes a public holiday in Scotland.

AD 973 A Viking invasion at Luncarty, near Perth, is thwarted, allegedly by thistles.

AD 995 Kenneth II killed, allegedly by a booby-trap.

1004 Two Scottish slaves arrive in the New World.

1010 Malcolm II uses Viking skulls to build a church at Mortlach, Banffshire.

1018 Northumbria becomes part of the kingdom of Alba (until 1030).

1034 Duncan I becomes king of Alba.

1040 Macbeth defeats Duncan and becomes king.

1057 Macbeth killed at Lumphanan by Malcolm Canmore, who becomes King Malcolm III. Exercises by Malcolm's troops at Braemar may have given rise to annual Highland Games.

1066 Scots and English co-operate to defeat a Viking invasion of Yorkshire. Norman conquest of England. English Princess Margaret escapes to Scotland and marries Malcolm III c.1068.

1072 Normans invade Scotland and force Malcolm III to accept English overlordship.

1093 Death of Malcolm and Margaret.

1098 Magnus Barelegs takes control of Hebrides and Mull of Kintyre.

1124 David I invites English and Normans to Scotland as his allies. The name 'Scotland' is now coming into use.

1136 Aberdeen Harbour Board founded – Scotland's oldest surviving business.

1174 William the Lyon is defeated by Henry II of England and is forced to accept Henry as his overlord.

1189 William regains independence in exchange for supporting English king Richard I's Crusading ambitions.

1263 Alexander III defeats a Viking fleet at Largs. Kingdom of Alba now includes most of modern Scotland except Orkney and Shetland.

1272 Edward I, 'Hammer of the Scots', becomes king of England.

1286 Accidental death of Alexander III.

1290 Death of Alexander's heir, Margaret, the 'Maid of Norway'.

1292 John Balliol becomes King of Scots, with Edward I of England as his overlord.

1295 Balliol makes an alliance with France against England.

1296 Edward I invades Scotland and defeats Balliol. He seizes southern Scotland and the Stone of Destiny.

1297 Scots under William Wallace and Sir Andrew Murray defeat Edward I at Stirling Bridge.

1298 Battle of Falkirk: English longbows inflict heavy casualties on the Scots.

1305 Wallace is betrayed to the English and hung, drawn and quartered. Robert the Bruce becomes King of Scots.

1306 Bruce murders his rival, Red John Comyn. Following a series of defeats by the English, Bruce goes into hiding.

1307 Death of Edward I.

1314 Scots under Bruce defeat Edward II at Bannockburn.

1320 Declaration of Arbroath demands Scotland's freedom from England.

1328 Peace between England and Scotland.

1329 Robert the Bruce dies of leprosy.

1338 'Black Agnes' Randolph defends the castle of Dunbar against an English siege.

1346 David II invades England and is taken prisoner. Stewart family comes to prominence in Scotland.

1349–1392 Major outbreaks of Black Death in Scotland.

Index

Things get even more peculiar in:

ᏚCOTLAND
A Very
Peculiar
History

Volume 2:
From the Stewarts
to modern Scotland

'God help England if she had no
Scots to think for her!'
George Bernard Shaw (Irish, 1856–1950)

The Cherish Family

The Cherish Brothers
at university

'The Cherished Library' is a definitive collection of masterworks, beautifully written, designed and illustrated by the most influential authors, artists, designers and bookbinders of their day.

These facsimile editions from the world-class collection of the Cherish family library have been lovingly crafted to recreate the authentic look and feel of the originals in the family's much-loved library.*

*The Cherished Library is a brand-new series designed to look and feel like classic books from a distinguished library, complete with fine bindings, library cataloguing notes and rich endpapers. The Cherished Library holds surprises...a must for collectors.